THE ARCHANGEL GUIDE TO ENLIGHTENMENT AND MASTERY

First published in the United Kingdom by:
The Sixth Floor, Watson House, 54 Baker Street, London W1U 7BU
Phone: +44 (0)20 3927 7290; Fax: +44 (0)20 3927 7291;
www.hayhouse.co.uk

Published in the United States of America by:
Hay House Inc., PO Box 5100, Carlsbad, CA 92018-5100
Tel: (1) 760 431 7695 or (800) 654 5126
Fax: (1) 760 431 6948 or (800) 650 5115; www.hayhouse.com

Published in Australia by:
Hay House Australia Ltd, 18/36 Ralph St, Alexandria NSW 2015
Tel: (61) 2 9669 4299; Fax: (61) 2 9669 4144; www.hayhouse.com.au

Published in India by:
Hay House Publishers India, Muskaan Complex, Plot No.3, B-2,
Vasant Kunj, New Delhi 110 070
Tel: (91) 11 4176 1620; Fax: (91) 11 4176 1630; www.hayhouse.co.in

The information given in this book should not be treated as a substitute for professional medical advice; always consult a medical practitioner. Any use of information in this book is at the reader's discretion and risk. Neither the authors nor the publisher can be held responsible for any loss, claim or damage arising out of the use, or misuse, of the suggestions made, the failure to take medical advice or for any material on third party websites.

A catalogue record for this book is available from the British Library.

ISBN: 978-1-4019-6589-1

Interior images: Robby Donaghey (www.artisticgenius.com)

Printed in the United States of America.

THE ARCHANGEL GUIDE TO ENLIGHTENMENT AND MASTERY

Living in the Fifth Dimension

DIANA COOPER AND **TIM WHILD**

HAY HOUSE

Carlsbad, California • New York City
London • Sydney • New Delhi

Contents

List of Visualizations

Introduction

For many years Tim Whild and I have worked individually and together with the awesome Archangel Metatron and so we were thrilled when he asked us to write *The Archangel Guide to Enlightenment and Mastery*.

Enlightenment is about seeing everything from a higher and wider perspective. When we learn to do this, we know that there is only love, for all else is illusion. This deep knowing transforms our entire way of being and all our relationships.

Mastery means taking responsibility for everything that happens to us. It is goodbye to guilt, blame, hurt and anger, and as we draw back all the energy we have invested in those emotions, we reclaim our power. A master stands strong and tall and acts from their inner wisdom.

In the time of Golden Atlantis, all the inhabitants were fifth-dimensional. They were enlightened masters – wise, gifted beings. But for the last 10,000 years, since Atlantis degenerated, people on Earth have been third-dimensional and have not felt accountable for either their actions or their emotions.

We are now experiencing a 20-year window of opportunity, as a new Golden Age is being set up on Earth and the frequency of the planet is rising rapidly to the level it was in Atlantis. We are living in extraordinary times, for those who are ready are being offered unprecedented spiritual promotion.

We start this book with chapters on the fascinating Golden Era of Atlantis, for the way they lived then forms the foundation of our enlightened mastery and the way humanity will live in the future. The information given here will trigger deeply hidden memories and open up your unconscious knowing.

The people in Golden Atlantis were in contact with their dragons, angels and unicorns. It is time to connect with them again. Beautiful and wise dragons are returning to Earth to help us, so we will introduce the fourth-dimensional elemental dragons here as well as the fifth-dimensional ones, for they are all our great friends, companions and protectors.

In addition, seventh and ninth-dimensional unicorns are pouring onto the planet now to assist us and to speed up our rate of spiritual growth. Touching the energy of these wonderful beings will bring you joy, love and inspiration. They help you to live in the fifth dimension.

We asked some of the great Illumined Masters and goddess masters to step forwards to shine their light through these pages. They have walked the ascension path on Earth and gone through their own trials and initiations, so they well understand the challenges we are undergoing. As they connect with us, they trigger the keys and codes of enlightenment and mastery that are latent within us. We offer them heartfelt thanks. With their help, we can receive much light and also serve the world.

One of these masters is Lord Kuthumi, the luminous being who is now World Teacher. He has set up 12 Halls of Learning on the inner planes. When you enter these, you receive information, light and energy codes that enable you to become an enlightened master in this lifetime.

Because the frequency is rising so rapidly, your chakra system is lighting up and expanding at an unprecedented rate. So we are including new information, at a higher vibration than ever before, to accelerate the spin and capacity of your 12 fifth-dimensional chakras.

We do hope you enjoy the new high-frequency information we have included and that you connect to the energies that pour through the visualizations at the end of each chapter.

We wish you joy on your journey to becoming a fully enlightened master.

May the dragons, angels, unicorns and Illumined Masters bless you and light up your life.

The Future of Our Mastery

CHAPTER 1

Masters of Earth

Mastery is the ability to control your energy systems and maintain your high frequency whatever is happening to you. 'Walking mastery' is a term applied to those who are living in a physical body while maintaining the upper levels of the fifth dimension. This occurs when you contain a high percentage of light in your four-body system – your physical, emotional, mental and spiritual bodies. This light is drawn into your aura when you pass tests and initiations sent to you by your soul.

It is possible for everybody on Earth right now to become an enlightened ascended master. Your decision to achieve this depends on your personal intention as well as your soul contract. In the current climate of possibilities, the seven billion people on this planet can all reach this level. This opportunity for fast spiritual promotion is unique to the current time and to this planet.

The blueprint for walking mastery has been provided by the 1,500-year Golden Era of Atlantis. The people of that time demonstrated how it could be done and their example is one of the foundations of this book. The information we need is encoded in each one of us who had an incarnation during that period.

In that Golden Era, the High Priests and Priestesses lived on the upper levels of the fifth dimension. They were in constant communication with seventh-dimensional beings and were able to live for very short periods in the sixth dimension. However, even those extraordinarily evolved beings could not maintain this level for long while occupying a physical body. At the sixth dimension they had to manage the energies around them with the power of the mind and the assistance of crystals.

Everybody, whatever their level, including children, undertook mind control training in the Golden Era of Atlantis in order to maintain the physical life they envisaged around them. This was done without ego and this was what allowed them to be walking masters.

Ascension from the third dimension involves building a pure crystalline light body, known as a merkabah. This is the geometric form created by your energies and your soul blueprint. When your 12 fifth-dimensional chakras are fully active, your soul beams down a tetrahedron to hold your physical vibration. This is made up of two interlocking pyramids, forming a three-dimensional six-pointed star. The next stage is when you balance your divine masculine energy with the divine feminine, and at this point your merkabah becomes a ball, for the circular shape, without corners, can hold more light.

The phase we are moving into now involves an expansion of the existing light bodies of all those in the fifth dimension. The chakras become translucent, losing their individual colours as they shimmer with the spectrum of white light, and a unified column of light is created, expanding from the heart centre in both directions. The heart chakra is the core of the ascension process driving the path of mastery. As the heart becomes stronger, the ego starts to lose its control and becomes obsolete. This happens when the master has passed the soul tests of the heart. These are crucifixions chosen before incarnation.

Each of the 12 chakras contains heart energy and an individual growth programme planned before birth. This creates a very challenging pathway for those dedicated to seeking enlightenment. Earth is by far the fastest and toughest school in the entire cosmos. However, the spiritual rewards are vast and prized beyond our comprehension throughout the universes.

In order to incarnate on this planet your soul must be at least a seventh-dimensional frequency. This may drop dramatically as you go through the Veil of Amnesia into a physical body and start your learning process. For some, it continues to reduce as karma is balanced from previous existences. Many souls are choosing this particular lifetime to redress all lessons and clear out everything before the start of the new Golden Age. This is one reason why the people on Earth appear to be having such different and difficult experiences now.

When you have learned from and overcome these lessons and experiences, incredible changes occur. The heart initiates the human process and pushes it forwards. As this happens, the consciousness of the soul evolves. You want to pursue a lifestyle that is loving, co-operative, sharing and interconnected with the whole of humanity.

This expanded outlook allows you as a master to be aware of who you really are. You know that you are spirit in a human form. This realization alone completely changes every aspect of your life, as then you bring Christ consciousness into every thought, word and deed. These changes are occurring now in people worldwide. It is predicted by the Intergalactic Council that by 2032 the entire vibration of Earth and its inhabitants will be fifth-dimensional.

Although the process of mastery affects all souls as individuals, it is a group operation. This is because every soul who wakes up from the heart affects the energetic state of everyone and everything around them. Also, heart communication between sentient and non-sentient life forms on Earth happens instantaneously. A master radiates an open heart and this allows one with a closed heart to see the reflection of who they truly are. As they see this reflection, the facets of their own heart can awaken. So, masters create masters, simply by being in their purest essence.

Walking mastery is the divine heritage of every soul on Earth.

In the coming years there will be new waves of sudden awakenings as people everywhere are touched by the rise in dimensional vibration. Unlike the initial wave of humans who have awakened slowly since the Harmonic Convergence in 1987, these newly conscious souls will find themselves in their chosen roles overnight.

To become a walking master, you must undergo and pass a considerable number of challenges and initiations. For those who have been waking slowly, this has been a long process. A rapidly awakened master, however, will have worked through their tests unconsciously. To these souls, understanding and realization come instantly. They instinctively embrace the universal flow as the true workings of Source become reality. Energy and information are immediately channelled to them via the fifth-dimensional heart chakra, offering a higher angelic perspective. As the ego takes a back seat for the first time since the fall of Atlantis, all illusion will be dispelled, to be replaced by enlightenment.

With the process of ascension fully underway, many masters are now remembering the souls with whom they shared their previous incarnations. Vast soul groups, all coming from the same monads, original divine sparks, are drawing together to anchor their soul light into powerful pools of energy. Working together instinctively, these clusters of people are drawing higher spectrums of Source light into the specific areas where they live. This is speeding up the higher vibration of the planet and allowing it to be fully anchored.

This in turn is clearing large bands of collective karmic energy from countries that need purification. When the souls working in this way consciously focus their intention on this vision, it speeds the process yet further.

Earth and its inhabitants are starting to remember the real meaning of the power of love.

Constantly standing by are the higher forces. As Illumined Masters of Earth, their role is becoming one of gentle guidance rather than full interaction. At the same time, the frequency bands within which humans and the angelic realms operate are becoming closer. This is making it easier for Earth and all on it to ascend.

Visualization to Prepare the World for Ascension

1. Choose a quiet and peaceful place and light a candle if you can.
2. Invoke your soul group, all those who originate from the same monad, to surround you. Have a sense of the many beautiful energies who are with you, supporting you.
3. Together you are part of a multi-coloured flame of intense and glorious light.
4. Allow this flame to anchor in a part of the world that is calling you.
5. Know that you are helping to clear and prepare the world for ascension.
6. Then step from the flame as an individual again.
7. Be aware of light shining from your heart and radiating in all directions.
8. You are one of the Brotherhood/Sisterhood of Love. You see and spread Christ consciousness wherever you go.
9. Stand tall as a walking master.
10. Open your eyes and smile.

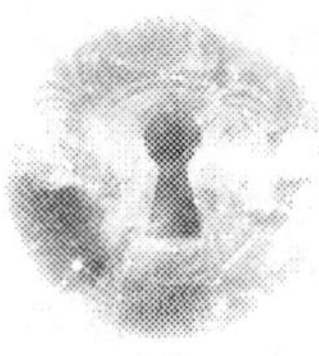

CHAPTER 2

The Next Step

The initial phase of the ascension energy has now been integrated into the planet. At first this energy illuminated the aura of Earth. This is the crystalline matrix surrounding the planet, reflecting the fifth-dimensional vibration at which we now resonate. As the frequency of our planet rises, every sentient being is affected by it, including humans. Through harmonic resonance, the energetic and spiritual construction of a human being must keep pace with this transformation. Many are now feeling this and it is changing their lives, though they may not be aware of the reason for it.

Once this transformation starts to occur, the fifth-dimensional heart begins to illuminate and decisions are heart-centred. Now the soul presents the person with tests to ensure that their heart is fully in command. This is one reason why people are receiving so many challenges right now. It is a sign that they are ready to move to the next phase, as tough paths indicate high callings.

During 2015 many deep planetary shifts took place. The most significant was the opening of the Christ Gate of Lyra at the triple alignment of the Spring Equinox. This date saw a new Moon, a solar eclipse and a massive expansion of the spring energy of new beginnings.

Archangel Christiel accesses this universe through the star system of Lyra. He is overlighting the causal chakra of everyone on Earth. The causal is a transcendent chakra at the back of the head that enables people to connect closely to angels, unicorns and the spirit world. It holds divine feminine energy and draws light from the Moon to enable people to balance their masculine and feminine energies and feel at peace.

A small amount of Archangel Christiel's energy has been trickling through for some time, enough to enable the causal chakras of those who were ready to become anchored. Since 2015 a flood of Christiel's energy has poured through the stargate and this has resulted in the seven billion-plus people on Earth being able to anchor their causal chakra. This in turn has enabled every soul to access their 12-chakra column. Every single person on the planet is now poised to take the decision to step onto the golden ascension path.

The balancing of the masculine and feminine energies after 10,000 years of imbalance has created change within many individuals and social structures. Because more souls are functioning from the heart, the new fifth-dimensional paradigm of love, co-operation and caring is becoming established. We will see an acceleration of the growth of all those structures that are serving the planet and humanity. This will enable soul satisfaction and happiness to spread.

As the Christ Gate of Lyra opened, many seekers found that the fifth veil of illusion dissolved immediately. This veil is pink and is intimately connected with the heart centre. It dissolves when we are ready to hold unconditional love in our heart. It enables deep forgiveness and allows us to see situations and people from a higher perspective. When this veil has dissolved, we can access those past lives that will benefit us now in our ascension process. It also opens us up to connect with our soul family and draws these people to us.

For some individuals, this was a very subtle shift. Others were challenged, as everything was reorganized and realigned at a higher frequency. This happened because thousands of ninth-dimensional pure white luminous unicorns poured through the stargate when it opened to accelerate the ascension of humanity.

Unicorns vibrate between the seventh and ninth dimensions. At the Harmonic Convergence in 1987, people's ascension lights started to go on. The seventh-dimensional unicorns saw this and took the opportunity to slip through a crack in the Lyran gateway. Then they helped those people who had the light of service over their heads or who were pure in heart.

At the full opening of the Lyran stargate in 2015, ninth-dimensional unicorns gained access and flooded in to help those whose hearts were open. The effect of this was so powerful it enabled another 10 per cent of humanity to awaken to their ascension path. It also pushed many ascension aspirants from the golden ascension path to the higher-frequency diamond one. This enabled their diamond light codes to be activated and increased their opportunity for service in the multiverse.

Once this 10 per cent of humanity had awakened, the collective consciousness of the planet shifted to a higher octave, bringing forwards more peace movements and a greater affinity with the animal kingdom.

At the auspicious opening of the Lyran stargate, the collective energy rose high enough for the 13th skull from Atlantis, the amethyst skull, to reveal some of its knowledge from the spiritual realms. It spoke, revealing ancient Atlantean wisdom from the Halls of Amenti. The 13 crystal skulls contain all the ancient wisdom, technology and information of the golden years of Atlantis. This wisdom will be used to rebuild our society based on Atlantean principles but at a higher frequency for the new Golden Age. Society will be based on the Law of One.

In September 2015 there was a huge influx of crystalline diamond energy, which means that all actions taken on this planet will now be reflected back as instant karma. This applies to everyone and is forcing people to take responsibility for their thoughts, words and actions. Grace, intention, manifestation, instant karma, responsibility and finally unconditional love will be the building blocks for the new world. At this huge tipping point, many more people started to wake up.

The return of instant karma is the start of tough love on the part of the universe. Because all those who are allowed to incarnate must have souls that are at least seventh-dimensional, it is time for these souls to remember who they are and act accordingly. All those working within the old paradigm will connect with their hearts and will see the impact of what they are doing reflected in their everyday lives. When this happens, they will wake up and want to change.

This will mean that structures will change from within to align with the heart frequencies. All others will gently dissolve to make way for higher economic ethics.

As we move fully into the fifth dimension, all choices of polarity are being withdrawn from us. Love and integrity will be the way forwards. The souls on the diamond pathway are already awakened and ready to do their powerful work.

Following September 2015, another huge realignment took place to allow the light bodies of the Earth souls to integrate yet higher frequencies. This created a wave of planetary and personal cleansing that introduced a fresh approach to how souls viewed their lives. For the first time in 10,000 years, lightworkers had full access to their hearts for guidance. The opening and anchoring of the fifth-dimensional heart allowed the energies of truth and integrity to shine forth.

This marked the start of the New Age. Old ways are now being replaced by a unified society filled with heart-based individuals. The navel chakra that was once fully active in Atlantis shines brightly once again, providing a full spectrum of dimensional connections between souls. For example, human beings on Earth are now able to connect to other members of their soul group, even if they are on the other side of the universe. Previously time, space and distance were viewed as obstacles that could not be overcome.

The fifth-dimensional Golden Age will rapidly teach the masters of Earth how to be masters again, harnessing the energies of the cosmos to bring light and love to the planet.

Visualization to Create Your Perfect Future

1. Prepare for meditation and relax in your sacred space.
2. Hold a quartz crystal over your third eye (any clear crystal such as a citrine or amethyst will work too).
3. Visualize yourself stepping smoothly along your ascension pathway, your challenges behind you.
4. Feel your light and power flooding through your 12 chakras and light body, and see your team of angels and dragons flying alongside you.
5. Imagine you come to a blank white wall. At the foot of the wall there are pots of coloured paint.
6. In your mind's eye, paint a beautiful picture of the Earth as you wish it to be. This can be any scenario that you choose to place on the wall.
7. Be as precise and intricate as you please. This is *your* picture.
8. When it is complete, stand back and admire your work. What have you created?
9. When it is perfect, ask your angels and dragons to bless and amplify the energies of your work.
10. See yourself stepping into your picture and it becoming your unified reality. Thoughts are simply energy prior to manifestation.

11. Feel how wonderful it is to flow with the energies of your own creation. Ask your crystal to record the pictures from your mind's eye and hold them in the light
12. Open your eyes and smile. As a master, you are co-creating with the Divine.

CHAPTER 3

The Re-establishment of Atlantis

The Creation of Temples

When the fifth and final experiment of Atlantis started, the first thing that the volunteers did was to build a physical temple to give thanks. This later became the Temple of Love overseen by Aphrodite and Venus. But for some time, until they had established homes and tribes, they worshipped in the open air, looking to the stars for illumination and inspiration.

Their biggest priority was always connection with and gratitude to Source. This was how they maintained the purity, enlightenment and mastery that led to the Golden Era of Atlantis. Because that age is the template for our golden future, we have included this chapter about the foundation of their fifth-dimensional lives.

The civilization of Atlantis had already collapsed four times, and with it the land. However, the Temple of Poseidon, containing the Sphinx and the Great Crystal that was their power source, had survived. It had been left isolated and inaccessible, however, as it had been built on the highest point of the Atlantean continent. The High Priests and Priestesses were the only people who could access this holy place. They were able to manipulate gravity and levitate or fly to it. From it, they poured light, love, illumination and practical information onto the volunteers on the plains below to enable them to maintain their high frequency.

Eventually the people built wondrous, high-frequency, round temples in the centre of each community to reflect the love and illumination that were emitted from the Temple of Poseidon. Each temple represented a different facet of Atlantean life. They were the Temple of Love, the Temple of Sound, the Temple of Healing, the Temple of the Sun, the Temple of the Moon, the Temple of Truth, the Temple of Night, the Temple of Animals, the Temple of Wisdom and Knowledge, the Temple of the One True Light, the Temple of the Sea and the Temple of Nature. Some of these temples were built of crystal. They would all share their information with one another to assist with the establishment of the Atlantean communities.

Each of these temples was surrounded by clear running water to maintain a high frequency and each had its own black cat to hold the energy and help with crystal alignment and divine alchemy.

The Atlanteans of this time recognized that all creation came from Source but that ultimately they were responsible for everything within themselves. This is an understanding that the masters of today are absorbing now.

Because the Atlanteans had to learn everything from the beginning, they discovered a great deal and learned how to put it into practice for the highest good. Reading about each of their temples will trigger unconscious memories and codes within you that will expand your personal light.

The Temple of Love

This was built of rose quartz and attuned directly to the cosmic heart, Venus. The stream of light coming to it from Venus carried the keys and sacred geometric codes of Christ consciousness, so that all who gave thanks here were bathed in perfect love. This enabled their own heart chakras to align with the Christ Light and ascension frequencies of love.

This was overseen by the High Priestess, Lady Venus. The priests and priestess of this temple established the higher heart frequencies and were the first to achieve ascension during the fifth experiment. Lady Venus later incarnated as a High Priestess in charge of the Temple of Love.

The Temple of Sound

The High Priests and Priestesses taught the importance of sound to the early Atlanteans as a fast way of establishing and maintaining a very high frequency. Sound can change the frequency of a solid object and turn it into something beautiful with sonic resonance. This method was also used for healing.

Later the Atlanteans realized they could manipulate matter by applying sound vibrations to physical objects and with the use of mind control could make objects lighter or heavier. They used this technique to construct buildings that were so advanced that they are beyond our current capability and also to make stones heavy in order to sink wells.

Vast spiritual technologies came from this particular temple. The resonance of these technologies is now coming back to us via crystal and sound healing, but most of them are still beyond our comprehension.

The Temple of Healing

The Temple of Healing was built of quartz crystal infused with emerald. Archangel Raphael used the emerald to magnify his healing light when someone was very out of alignment. This would bring them into divine perfection.

The Temples of Sound and Healing collaborated closely. The priests and priestesses of these temples would harmonize their work to produce powerful methods of healing. Their intention was always to bring the person into alignment with their true divine blueprint.

At the peak of the Golden Era, there was no karma and if people went off-centre they only needed to be rebalanced. One of the priests or priestesses could easily do this.

Magnificent flawless crystals were energized by the Sun and Moon and the intentions of the healers. These light-filled crystals were then tapped or a harmonic hum was emitted by the healer. This released the sonic wave that brought the patient back into perfect alignment.

In addition, the beings of the Pleiades poured their blue rays and their knowledge into the temple crystals so that these vibrations could be released by the priesthood. The result was an incredibly powerful harmonic heart healing that immediately balanced the entire four-body system and allowed perfect physical alignment to take place.

As the Atlantean energy started to devolve, karma began to play a part and stronger healing was needed. All healing in the Temple of Healing was offered under grace, and while grace dissolves karma, the enlightened priesthood wanted to demonstrate the spiritual laws so that the patient would repay the cause of the disease in another way, often through service.

When the Golden Era was initiated, the High Priests and Priestesses taught the people about the medicinal use of herbs. Later the priesthood in charge of the Temple of Healing became herbal alchemists and people would arrive from far and wide to benefit from their expertise. They understood that every herb resonated with part of the body. When that herb was perfectly prepared, it contained the golden blueprint of that organ. This overlaid the body and brought the organ to its original divine perfection.

This method worked quickly and easily, for the people would only be slightly out of balance. In modern times, however, now karma has become entrenched, it works more slowly.

Powerful sacred geometric patterns were also created with crystals. The patient would lie on a couch and the grid would be laid around them and activated by the intention of the priest. The temple cat would usually watch over this. Sometimes the feline would move the crystals to ensure they were in perfect alignment. At others it would sit on the person to draw in the highest possible light.

At the peak of Golden Atlantis, highly advanced crystal technology allowed healers to place accident victims in crystal cocoons. Blessed water was then placed over the person and magnified by the high-frequency crystals. This had the power to heal instantly.

These crystal cocoons were also regeneration chambers and could extend the lives of those who wished to extend their service on Earth by pouring high-frequency light into their cells.

The Temple of the Sun

The Temple of the Sun was of great importance to the Atlanteans. They realized that the Sun was a portal to the higher dimensions that allowed a controlled flow of light to enter our known universe and integrate with the planet. It was an ode to the light that cascaded into the Great Crystal that powered Atlantis.

The Temple of the Sun was built using a mixture of very clear quartz, citrine and gold to assist with the highest level of light refraction. The temple also served to teach Atlanteans how to provide energy for themselves by harnessing the Sun's rays via crystals and copper-infused metal and distributing them throughout the Atlantean continent as power.

The priests and priestesses of this temple were directly connected to the light and teachings of Archangel Metatron.

He trained the High Priest Ra to apply his incredible knowledge to form the template for the 1,500-year Golden Era.

The Temple of the Sun was also tuned directly into the inflow and codings that were available from Suns in other universes. During the Golden Era, the temple would receive vast transmissions of pure light. This was then passed to others to assist with the rapid building of the cosmic ascension process throughout Atlantis. This is the level beyond fifth-dimensional ascension where souls transit into cosmic mastery of themselves and the universes around them.

The teachings of this temple were stored in a citrine master skull, which had a beautiful sunstone infused into its third eye. This incredibly advanced crystal technology was achieved by harnessing the knowledge of the Arcturians and using it to shape, melt and carve the crystal being used.

The Temple of the Moon

This temple was established by the High Priestess Isis and only the purest of the priestesses were allowed to enter it. It was made of moonstone and was a centre of divine feminine energy. It was crucial for keeping the balance between masculine and feminine exact.

The priestesses of the Moon would devote their entire lives to honouring the Moon's cycles and harvesting its light for distribution.

Archangel Christiel would assist with the flows of energy. This mighty archangel kept the temple informed when the light was wavering in parts of Atlantis so that adjustments could be made throughout the continent.

All the women who dedicated their incarnations to this beautiful temple worked in absolute harmony and co-operation with one another. Their bodies worked in perfect unison with the monthly cycles and they did everything for the highest good of all.

Within their temple was a crystal skull carved from shimmering moonstone.

When Atlantis fell for the final time, the Sisterhood of the Moon was re-established in ancient Egypt and the secrets of its light consigned to the safekeeping of the Sphinx.

The Temple of Truth

The Temple of Truth was constructed of pure white quartz to reflect the purity of Archangel Gabriel. Archangel Gabriel worked directly with the Atlanteans to assist them in bringing truth and order into their lives.

Such was the purity of this temple that the chakras of the priests glowed with an iridescent white light, indicating that they had evolved to the higher level of the fifth dimension. Truth is the integral core of a spiritual being and raises the vibration.

This temple brought transparency to everyone in Atlantis and allowed the people living there to exhibit complete honesty in all that they did and said.

The Temple of Night

The Temple of Night was honoured by the Atlanteans as an essential part of life on planet Earth. As spring follows winter, day follows night, and the evolved fifth-dimensional souls of Atlantis knew that they had nothing to fear from the darkness as it was a part of the Earth experience. Darkness holds the secrets of the divine feminine and it is here that true wisdom is found. The temple was therefore constructed from obsidian.

The priests and priestesses of this temple were experts in soul purity, as they continuously monitored their internal thoughts and feelings. When they identified emotions that were out of alignment with Source love, they handed them to the unicorns for purification.

Rituals to honour the dream state were performed daily to ensure that the priesthood of this temple always journeyed to the higher spiritual realms during sleep. They would travel with dragons as companions to safeguard their passage. When they returned to their bodies during the day, they brought great knowledge and sacred wisdom from the angelic realms.

The Temple of Animals

This temple honoured and revered all sentient beings. The Atlanteans knew that animals were special souls who incarnated on Earth from all parts of the universes. The animals of the Golden Era were all chosen for the Atlantean experiment to support the humans in their roles there.

Archangel Fhelyai oversaw the running of this temple. He regularly sent information to the priesthood on how to nurture the new waves of animals that came to Atlantis.

The children of Atlantis loved this temple and were always flocking to learn about the beautiful creatures who lived amongst them. Co-operation between species was taught from a very early age and children were shown how to honour and respect all life-forms.

The Temple of Wisdom and Knowledge

This highly revered temple honoured the soul wisdom of all beings. The High Priests and Priestesses knew that true wisdom came from many lifetimes of spiritual service filled with love. They believed that everyone had something to impart. The first lesson of this temple was to teach the priests and priestesses to listen properly.

The wisdom of many incarnations was stored in this temple in a quartz crystal, and the understandings of the different tribes were always pooled in order to expand their knowledge and to create balance. Information taught during the current incarnation was stored in a separate skull, and this was highly respected. Much of it was passed on by the Star Beings who connected with Earth and the elemental realms.

The Temple of the One True Light

This vast quartz temple was a pinnacle of technological advancement. Using crystal technology, it gathered light from all corners of the multiverse. This was then used to amplify the light bodies of the spiritual souls of Atlantis whenever they needed to make progress quickly.

Lord Voosloo, the highest-frequency High Priest ever to serve in Atlantis, worked directly with this temple and would often take new initiates there for their first galactic connections. He was able to fill their bodies with pure light and then direct their consciousness to connect to the stars. This enabled them to access and download inter-stellar knowledge and wisdom.

The greatest teaching of this temple was to show the Atlanteans their true essence. Those who experienced the temple under the direction of Lord Voosloo would be shown their infinite connection to All That Is.

The priests and priestesses of this temple used a highly conductive mixture of citrine and clear quartz to bring in higher vibrations from the Pleiades, Andromeda, Arcturus, Sirius, Lyra and many other stars, planets and galaxies. This light was collected in the crystals there so that the temple itself would glow in the dark.

All Atlanteans were honoured for the inner Sun that glowed within them.

The Temple of the Sea

This temple, also known as the Temple of Neptune, worked closely with the flowing waters of ascended Neptune, called

Toutillay. The priests and priestesses of this temple focused upon the ceaseless movement of energy from one space to another.

The Atlanteans understood that third dimensional energy formed objects and that higher-frequency energy flowed continuously in the form of liquid light. Initiates of the Temple of Neptune were trained to work with energies that were much higher than they were. They became experts in manifestation.

Neptune's energy always asked that inner as well as outer soul work be attended to. Tests would be set regularly to ensure that the priesthood were in touch with their deepest emotions, as these greatly affected the creations that they projected into the physical world.

The teachings of the Temple of Neptune were so sacred that at the fall of Atlantis they were returned to Neptune for protection. This light and information is now becoming available again to those who are truly ready to accept all aspects of their soul and are willing to work to the highest level.

The Temple of Nature

The Temple of Nature was one of the most beautiful structures of Atlantis. Set in glorious woodland, it was where all aspects of natural law were taught to show Atlanteans how to respect the spirit of the Earth. Lady Gaia and her elemental master, Taia, would work directly with the Higher Selves of all who visited this temple. They showed them how to honour and bless the land so that every footstep left a golden imprint.

Trees, plants, insects, birds and animals would be drawn to the vibration of this temple and the Atlanteans spent hours in psychic communication with them. They taught everyone how to live symbiotically with Earth life. Because the delicate balance of nature was honoured and all was kept in harmony, the Earth responded by producing a cornucopia of delight for them: high-frequency nutritious food, radiantly beautiful blooms and luscious green trees and grass.

The Temple of Poseidon

Sometimes known as the Cathedral of the Sacred Heights, this was the greatest and most spiritual of all of the temples of Atlantis. Built at the highest point on the Isle of Poseida, as mentioned earlier, this edifice was inaccessible to the Atlanteans until they had mastered the art of levitation. In the latter years of the Golden Era, the priesthood took the decision to open the temple to others by building a road to the top.

The great amethyst skull resided in this temple and the accumulated light, love and wisdom of all the skulls was stored within it. The great masters of Atlantis would spend time in this temple and the higher initiations would always be conducted here under the close supervision of the High Priests and Priestesses and guided by the Intergalactic Council.

At the fall of Atlantis, the secrets of Poseida were stored within the Halls of Amenti and are guarded to this day by the Legions of Anubis. (The Legions of Anubis are the workforce of the god Anubis. They all carry his love and high frequency, and act as his extension.) The reincarnated masters who have returned to Earth are just starting to remember how to retrieve this sacred knowledge. It is being used to shift the ascension process into a higher gear and to recreate the fifth-dimensional blueprint for Earth that was established in the Golden Era of Atlantis.

The way the Atlanteans lived, co-operated, shared and loved was the foundation for an ascended way of life. It formed the template for walking mastery on this planet. We are now remembering those times in order to bring the teachings back so that Earth can ascend fully into the fifth dimension and radiate golden light once more.

CHAPTER 4

Helping Children to Enlightenment and Mastery in Golden Atlantis

In the Golden Era of Atlantis, everything was undertaken from an enlightened perspective and all decisions were made from a point of mastery. Bringing a new soul into the world and educating them were considered to be incredibly important. The young person was being trained for enlightenment and mastery. We have much to learn from the people of this era about the importance and powers of parenting, which is why we are including this chapter here. When this pathway is undertaken with integrity, it offers many opportunities for enlightenment and mastery.

Parenthood was not for everyone. The Magi, that is, the higher priests, and most of the initiates were celibate. Only those who were ready for celibacy were allowed to undertake this highly evolved role. In addition, not all women were destined to be mothers. This decision was made at a soul level. Some chose to dedicate their lives to something else, such as creativity. Others devoted themselves to looking after the children of others, either caring for orphans or in a teaching capacity.

When you vibrate at the upper levels of the fifth dimension, as they did during this period, the masculine and feminine energies within you are perfectly balanced. Therefore sex was regarded as a sacred act for the purpose of procreation. If a couple fell in love and wanted to marry, they would first visit the local priest, who was highly evolved and psychically trained. The priest would examine the auras of the couple to check that they were physically, mentally, emotionally and spiritually compatible. If they were not, they would not marry. They would not want to! There would be no purpose in marriage if it were not for the highest good of all.

The Atlanteans were pragmatic and they knew that relationships were challenging. If a couple was not happy together, despite the precautions taken to ensure they were compatible, they could divorce without problem. This was, however, rare.

The wedding was a powerful ceremony calling in great spiritual powers to overlight the couple, but there was no exchange of rings or any other symbols, as this was not considered necessary.

The couple knew that one of the greatest spiritual responsibilities anyone could assume in a lifetime was to bring in a soul and that the task of caring for that child was considered to be vital. They also understood that parenting was high-frequency service work. So in order to prepare for this blessed task, they would meditate together, often with the extended family, to discover what kind of soul they could best serve. At this point two or three spirits might present themselves so that they could explore one another's energies and, before conception, a decision would be taken that would best serve everyone. The physical sexual act would draw in the new soul, who would then connect with the mother's body.

When the baby was born, they would be welcomed and greeted not just by the parents and immediate family but by the whole community. Every single baby was keenly awaited, warmly welcomed and hugely loved. They would be taken to the temple, where the priest would examine their aura to discover what their soul journey had been and what gifts and talents they were bringing into that life. This was enormously helpful to the child, for the parents and community were then able to honour and encourage the things they were good at. Every child blossoms when their good points are drawn out, and the children of the Golden Age of Atlantis were particularly blessed in this respect.

With their extraordinary powers, the Magi were able to draw in liquid crystal from the baby's planet of origin. This then solidified and became the child's personal birth crystal. It acted as a connection to the child's star or planet of origin and enabled the child to touch base energetically with their home. This, too, helped the child to feel connected and safe and to take an enlightened perspective on life. Even now you can choose a crystal you feel drawn to and ask it to connect you to your home planet. Place it under your pillow so that it can make the energetic link while you sleep. You may feel more comfortable and settled as the connection becomes stronger.

When the child was quite young, a lurcher puppy would arrive on their doorstep. This animal was expected and would become the child's companion, accompanying them to school and protecting them. In exchange the child learned to look after the canine. Lurchers carried the perfect blueprint for the 'dog' energy at that time. Their beautiful temperament and intelligence made them widely accepted.

Child and canine would always have a very close bond and the dog would remain until the child married or joined the priesthood at the age of 16. Then the pet had completed their mission and would return to spirit.

The presence of this canine companion throughout their formative years ensured that the child felt safe and protected.

It enabled their base and sacral chakras to glow, spin and radiate at a high frequency. This was an excellent foundation for mastery. As there were three children on average in each family, there were three lurchers also, which provided lots of fun, games and informality.

In addition each child had a rabbit. Rabbits originate from Orion, the planet of wisdom. They come to Earth with huge missions, part of which is to be heart healers. If a child was upset, they would cuddle their soft, furry rabbit, and the rabbit would heal them with love and wisdom. This enabled the children of Atlantis to keep their hearts fully open and operational at all times. This, too, is a wonderful foundation for loving walking mastery.

When the children were about three they were taken in small groups into nature, where they learned about the natural and spiritual world. Their teachers were dedicated and chosen for their innate ability to relate to children of that age. As the youngsters delved into the secrets of nature, they were encouraged to look at life with enlightened eyes.

Even at this age, the children were taught to concentrate, focus and use their imagination, as this was the perfect basis for the mind control techniques that they would learn when they were old enough to manifest and create.

Whatever the age of the child, there was a huge emphasis on relaxation. Schools were places of calm and happiness. Games, fun, music and special breathing techniques enabled children to relax so that they could absorb information very easily. Education literally means drawing out your latent talents, and this was the intention of the teachers for their charges.

When the children were older, they would practise relaxing down to a cellular level. This allowed the beads or codons in their 12 strands of DNA to stretch out and touch each other perfectly. This connection enabled them to access their full potential.

The Atlanteans did not try to force other people's knowledge into children's minds; rather, they focused on allowing the child's gifts, talents and soul knowledge to surface naturally. Each individual was encouraged to do what they loved to do most. In this way they grew up to be happy and fulfilled at a soul level.

The only teaching of information that was allowed came through high-frequency quartz crystals that were programmed with spiritual knowledge. When they were older, the children were taught how to access this directly or through their own individual teaching quartz crystals.

Because everyone was telepathic, language was rudimentary and there was no interest in grammar. Everyone communicated mind to mind with thoughts or pictures. They created these with intention in their third eye and passed them from their third eye to someone else's. For example, if you wanted to know what your child was doing, you sent a telepathic message and in response you received a picture or video from that child's mind directly into your own.

Creativity, art and music are right-brain activities, so these were encouraged. So too was sport, as it was considered important to take responsibility for the body and keep it healthy. Pure water, lovingly grown and blessed vegetarian food, and happiness were the ingredients for mastery of the body.

Here is a visualization to assist you in taking responsibility for your personal frequency.

Visualization to Draw Out the Gifts of Your Inner Child

1. Prepare a space where you can be relaxed and undisturbed. Light a candle if you can.
2. Sit quietly and breathe comfortably with the intention of drawing out the gifts of your inner child.
3. Focus upon your activated Earth Star.
4. Ask Archangel Michael to place his deep blue cloak of protection around you.
5. Imagine you are three years old, playing happily in a beautiful woodland glade with a gentle brown dog.
6. You are aware of elementals fluttering in the grass and trees, and radiant angels watching you.
7. A wise teacher sits under a tree and you joyfully run over to her.
8. She tells you all your good points. She reminds you of your gifts and talents. She may even tell you some you are not consciously aware of.
9. She hands you your own personal birth crystal. It may be any colour and a different shape from any you may have imagined. As you hold it, whether you are aware of it or not, a link is forming to your home star or planet, even if it is in another universe.
10. Sense yourself relaxing as feelings of belonging, safety, self-worth and hope bubble inside you.
11. Open your eyes and bring yourself into the present, with these good feelings growing and expanding inside you.

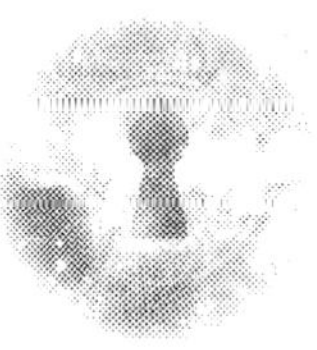

CHAPTER 5

The Return of the Enlightened Masters and the Halls of Amenti

The Harmonic Convergence in 1987 saw the return of enlightenment to Earth. When Atlantis fell, spiritual energies such as the Violet Flame and the Mahatma were withdrawn to ensure that they were only handled by those whose hearts remained pure. While purity exists in the hearts of all the souls of Earth, most have forgotten how to access it. Only certain souls have carried their light brightly enough for the higher forces and the Intergalactic Council to see it from the illumined dimensions. But this has been enough to ensure that the energies returned to the planet.

Such is the importance of the ascension process that everything that is occurring now was planned 260,000 years ago at the start of the Atlantis experiment. As a result, soul groups of highly trained ascended masters agreed to incarnate at the same time on Earth. They all agreed to go through the Veil of Amnesia to forget their origins. This is comprised of seven levels of illusion. It ensures that every single one of these masters comes to Earth to live life in very human circumstances. Only then can they be expected to teach and lead the millions of rapidly awakening souls into the new Golden Age of Aquarius. You may well be one of them.

In the past millennia, many of these masters have achieved great pinnacles of spiritual enlightenment in other incarnations or on the inner planes. This has aroused huge feelings of expectation, and beings from all corners of the universes have gathered to witness and support the shift that is occurring. They are all helping in their special and unique manner.

Every master who has incarnated holds a vital key to the process. Each brings in a unique spectrum of gifts and talents that harmonizes with the light of the others in their soul group. This creates a vast and powerful unit of masters dedicated to the highest light.

Soul groups start drawing together and unifying as soon as key members of the team are awake. Masters from Atlantis, Lemuria, Egypt and all other evolved civilizations are now remembering who they were and with whom they were connected in previous lives.

These connections are incredibly powerful. They draw souls to relocate and change their circumstances when they feel the urge to do so. Then they can operate energetically as a team, even when they do not consciously know each other. They are here to hold, bolster and illuminate the first wave of the ascension process and lead the way with love.

As the second wave started to build momentum in September 2015, the core groups took leadership roles in preparation for the physical shifts in the structures of society.

Before 2012 civilizations such as the Mayans foresaw the end of the world. But what the Mayans really saw was a blank page after the Cosmic Moment on 21 December 2012.

The high-frequency priesthood could not scry into the era beyond Atlantis, which ended at the Cosmic Moment. Most predictions for this period were channelled and written by souls carrying a third-dimensional vibration. You cannot read into a vibration above yours, and this means that their predictions were distorted and are not valid. The future is now entirely influenced by the people of Earth, especially the ascended masters.

Love and positive creation are the most important jobs for the awakened masters. They have agreed to help open people's hearts by opening their own.

With the knowledge and love of those already awakened on Earth, a vast web of light has now anchored globally. This has been made easy by social media, which has enabled spiritual groups from opposite sides of the planet to pool their energies at the touch of a button. Support groups for advanced and beginners alike regularly meet to take responsibility for their spiritual growth. New waves of masters are stepping forwards as this vibration increases and grows.

When a certain percentage of these beings are awake, the higher realms will step back and allow them to make their own decisions. One of the most important facets of mastery is self-reliance.

Many of these souls have woken up overnight. They have chosen to do so at precisely the right time and place. They are easy to recognize, as they have a vast and immediate understanding of the workings of the universe.

Every master who has served Earth in a significant lifetime has come to help and as a result the golden light from the Earth is now clearly visible from the higher dimensions. These lightworkers are now starting to use knowledge from the Halls of Amenti to speed up the ascension process.

The Halls of Amenti

The Halls of Amenti are a vast cosmic library held in the higher realms. They were created by the universal angels to record the spiritual achievements of all the known universes.

The Halls of Amenti differ from the Akashic records, as these are used to log the life experiences of those incarnating on Earth. Many gifted spiritual mediums have access to the Akashic records, but they can only access information that matches their vibration. Those who vibrate at a higher level are able to delve deeply into the more illuminated history of a soul. However, it should be noted that sometimes access to these records is deliberately blocked by the guides and angels of the person involved, because past-life information can often be distracting if it is not relevant to the soul mission.

The halls are an ascended space filled with light and love. All the masters from all the reaches of time and space have their own rooms there and the information within each room expands as the soul progresses on their chosen pathway.

The Legions of Anubis were created to guard these spaces and they do so very carefully.

At the fall of Atlantis, many of the masters rushed to fill the halls with their information before it fell into the wrong hands. Technology and spiritual tools from the Golden Era of Atlantis are becoming accessible again now that the vibration on Earth is rising.

There are several entrance points to the halls. One is found via Agartha, which is the capital city of Hollow Earth, while another is directly below the feet of the Sphinx. Some say that the vibration of the halls can be felt very clearly from this spot. There is also access from the great pyramids of Tibet, Greece, Mesopotamia and Machu Picchu and from the Mayan one.

The Halls of Amenti are a stunning sight to behold. At the entrance there is a golden doorway, followed by a long golden tunnel lit by torches. Once a person has entered this tunnel, their ascension pathway accelerates and they take their higher tests. After passing these initiations, they stand at the guarded gates of the first level. The Sentinels of Anubis scan the light body of the soul to assess their vibration and allow them to pass.

The first level of Amenti looks like a vast room. Within this room are the names of all of the masters who serve the universes. This space stretches for as far as the eye can see, lit by torches of liquid gold. Beautiful seats of contemplation line the room so that visitors may rest and absorb the beautiful frequencies.

At the end of the room stand two golden sentinels guarding the entrance to the master chambers. A soul must have passed their initiations on Earth to enter. Some masters can stand at this doorway for many years before they gain access, and their initiations are always challenging.

Once the doors are open the master gains access to the second level, which is a golden pyramid filled with spiritual heritage. Some choose to use this room as their retreat and travel to Amenti in their sleep to work on various projects.

The mysteries of Hollow Earth are kept in the third level of Amenti. This level is still connected to the Earth energies, but it is vast and can take lifetimes to explore. Serapis Bey holds his White Ascension Flame in this seventh-dimensional space.

The fourth level is connected to the galactic masters. This is the hall that contains the knowledge of the extraterrestrials and universal angels and is eighth or ninth-dimensional in vibration.

The fifth level is dedicated to Cosmic Universal Wisdom. Source touches this 10th-dimensional level.

The sixth level is relatively unexplored by the human mind, but is said to contain the light and love of the stars themselves. Ascended master Thoth attempted to access this level during his sleep, but was told he had to progress further in his own universe first. This level is vibrates at the 11th dimension and sometimes touches the 12th.

The seventh level is filled with pure Source Light. This is then passed to the Seraphim and the Dragons of Creation as they build new universes with light and love. This hall vibrates at a 12th-dimensional frequency in alignment with Source.

Visualization to Connect to the Halls of Amenti

1. Prepare for meditation. Focus on the Halls of Amenti during the day and set your intention to visit them.
2. Choose a space where you will be undisturbed and light a candle if you wish.
3. Call the Legions of Anubis to seal your sacred space and guide you to the entrance of Amenti.
4. Stand by the gates and state your intention to enter. Feel the golden resonance flowing from this sacred space.
5. As the gates open, walk through with your sentinel companions.
6. A golden angel awaits you on the other side. This is your guardian angel, who has assisted you in the progress of your soul journey since it started.
7. Your angel leads you down a vast tunnel lit with torches of liquid gold. Ancient symbols of love and wisdom adorn the walls. Some of them may seem familiar to you.
8. Your angel stops at the end of this tunnel and asks you to place your hand upon the golden doorway at the end.
9. The doorway is the entrance to your master room. Allow your light to flow from your hand to open the doorway.
10. You step inside the room. Here is a vast space filled with the achievements of many lifetimes. You will have records that span every incarnation throughout the universe.
11. There is a gift in this room that you have kept here for yourself. It is contained within a golden box with your current name on it.

12. Open the box. What gift are you giving yourself now for your ascension pathway?
13. With the help of your angel, place this gift within your heart and absorb its incredible energy.
14. Leave your room in Amenti now and remember that you can return here anytime you wish.
15. Return to your sacred space and thank your angel and the Sentinels of Anubis.
16. Open your eyes and use your gift to enhance your ascension process here on Earth.

The Expanded Chakras

CHAPTER 6

The Expanded Earth Star Chakra

During the third-dimensional phase of evolution on Earth, the seven-chakra column played its role of limited connection perfectly. Humans wandered the planet gazing at the stars and pondering their existence. Their connection to their Source energy had to be discovered along the way. Many lost their connection. However, this is changing. Once a person's Earth Star is activated, everything changes.

Depending on your perspective, the Earth Star is either the first or the last chakra in the 12-chakra column. The development of this chakra is carefully monitored by Archangel Sandalphon. Because of the vital role that it is playing in the progress of the planet, he will offer continual support throughout your soul's incarnation on Earth. The archangels of the other chakras do not do this.

At the very beginning of the ascension process the Earth Star can be seen as an inert ball of black and white energy. As it wakes up, it takes on a deep grey colour, reflecting the magnetic substances of the planet's crust. This enables it to start its grounding connection to the mother essence of Gaia, the spirit of Earth. When this energy circuit starts to flow, the soul on the ascension pathway never needs to ground their energy again.

In the third dimension, grounding was an everyday part of spiritual life. The aspirant would always remember to ground their energy in the morning, just as they would clean their teeth regularly. Lightworkers who were very sensitive had to work hard to keep their four-body system in one place.

Grounding also unifies the body into a single column of resonant light. The Earth Star's connection to the planetary magnetics and energy field does this job automatically.

As your soul progresses through the primary ascension stage, your Earth Star expands in size and power. Its role is to guide you to the location allocated for your mission. When you are born, your fifth-dimensional chakra blueprint is programmed with the content of the life mission for your master self. So your Earth Star knows exactly where you are supposed to be on the planet.

Now that the initial process of cleansing has been completed, many souls are feeling the freedom within their hearts to follow their chosen path. When they are unified with their chosen spot, their personal energy will rise dramatically. Souls who have not yet fully settled will feel restless until they do so.

This is a very powerful process and very often your soul is not aware of it until you have reached your destination. Then your Earth Star turns to liquid silver and reflects the ninth-dimensional light of Archangel Sandalphon himself.

Some lightworkers talk of amazing journeys of the heart that they have taken without any thought or logic. They step onto a boat or plane to visit a faraway land or sacred site that is calling to them. Or they feel a great desire to live in a certain country and they find themselves there.

When this happens to you, your Earth Star is working at its most powerful level. When you reach the chosen site, this chakra will download specific light codes into the planet to activate it at a higher frequency. These journeys will continue to be a vital part of the establishment of the Golden Age here on Earth. Many masters who are pulled to a certain place have already spent powerful lifetimes there. They are returning to finish work that was planned many lifetimes ago.

The ascended master Thoth used his Earth Star to its maximum capacity during the Golden Era of Atlantis. Following the fall, he channelled vast pools of light from the higher realms into the planetary ley system to maintain the integrity of the Christ consciousness. This was achieved by drawing in light from the galactic Suns via his Stellar Gateway and passing it down through his feet in concentrated streams. This energy was focused and amplified by the gridding of specific crystals and crystal skulls. Many lightworkers have now remembered how to achieve this and are performing similar tasks in locations all over planet Earth.

The Earth Star is also assisting the awakened souls to keep pace with the rising frequency on Earth. As the vibration of Lady Gaia rises, the frequency of the people on Earth automatically rises with it. So we are forced to progress too, and unconsciously have to work hard to align with the new frequency. This is one of the ways in which the ascension of the planet is being accelerated.

The Earth Star is also deeply connected to the seventh-dimensional kingdom of Hollow Earth. Here Serapis Bey works in his Great Golden Crystal Pyramid. Within it he holds the connection for every single Earth Star chakra on the planet. He grounds the energy of all these chakras into this vast source of light.

As the Golden Crystal Pyramid becomes more accessible to lightworkers, they draw the higher codes of the five Golden Ages on Earth (Angala, Petranium, Mu, Lemuria and Atlantis) into their chakra column. This provides them with information that is essential for their pathways. As the ascension process on Earth evolves, this ancient knowledge will become a part of everyday life once again.

Visualization to Expand the Earth Star

1. Prepare for meditation. Find a sacred space where you will be undisturbed.
2. Ask the fire dragons to clear completely your four-body system of any density. Invite them to clear your Earth Star chakra also.
3. Relax as these mighty beings work within and around you.
4. When you are pure and clear, invoke Archangel Metatron. Ask him to run a column of light from the Great Central Sun down through your 12 chakras into Hollow Earth.
5. Relax as the golden-orange light floods through you.
6. Bring your attention to your Earth Star chakra. Invoke Archangel Sandalphon and ask him to illuminate it with his bright silver light.
7. See your Earth Star glowing with silver threads connecting you to the energies of Mother Earth. Allow this silver light to flow into the cells of your body, unifying you completely.
8. Call on Serapis Bey to light up the Golden Crystal Pyramid with the ancient light codes for your spiritual mission.
9. Allow your Earth Star to connect with the Golden Pyramid and see Serapis Bey drawing the light of your chakra into his beautiful crystal skull.
10. Light codes and information are now travelling up to your Earth Star. Be ready to receive and integrate them in whatever way they present themselves.
11. Now allow your Earth Star to connect with the planetary Earth Star chakra in London, UK.
12. Allow your light to flow to this spot, raising its vibration even higher.

13. When you feel ready, thank Archangels Sandalphon and Metatron. Thank Master Serapis Bey and the dragons too.
14. Open your eyes and be ready to spread light wherever your feet touch the ground.

CHAPTER 7

The Expanded Base Chakra

The fifth-dimensional base chakra is the anchor point for our ascended mastery. It is sometimes described as the seat of the soul and enables us to achieve spiritual enlightenment.

When we embody our higher aspects, we begin our ascension process and this chakra glows with bright platinum light. Archangel Gabriel is responsible for the nurturing of the base chakra in the early stages of its development and assists us in purifying the lower energies that it may contain.

In the third dimension, the base chakra glowed a deep red. This colour represented the survival emotions that were experienced here on Earth, and many souls became lost within their lessons. As a result of this, many people began looking to often flawed leaders and teachers to make them feel safe. This is now rapidly changing as the platinum light of faith, trust, joy and harmony flows into our base chakras, attracting happy circumstances.

When Earth began her ascension process, we were able to reconnect with our mighty I AM Presence, our divine spark. This prompted many lightworkers to begin to anchor the higher aspects of themselves into their four-body system. When the fifth-dimensional base chakra is fully anchored, it expands until the division between Higher and Lower Self ceases to exist. We become our Higher Self.

As our light rises and we begin our master pathway here on Earth, the base chakra draws the vibration of the soul directly into the body. There are millions of people who have now achieved this transition. However, they do not realize it until they embrace their true magnificence.

The base chakra frequency tries to draw to our attention an understanding of who we truly are and this is one of the commonest lessons that it is teaching us on the master pathway.

Our emotional body is part of our four-body system and holds the memories of our lives in a physical body. Archangel Gabriel has recently combined his pure light with that of Archangel Christiel to help us clear our emotional bodies very quickly. Working together for the highest good of Earth and humanity, they have created a mixture of the Diamond Ray of Purification and the Cosmic Christ Light that is released for us at every full Moon.

This act of grace has enabled another wave of lightworkers to enter the second phase of the ascension process and embody a vibration that was available in Golden Atlantis. The mighty fire dragons have been assisting Archangel Gabriel with this mission, and they work ceaselessly on a 24-hour basis to ensure that we maintain the purest vibrations in our base chakras.

After every succeeding full Moon, a higher energy becomes available to us and our base chakras can anchor it. This process also strengthens our Antakarana bridge, which connects us directly to our monad in the higher dimensions.

Memories of the Golden Era of Atlantis are beginning to remind us of who we truly are. Many aspirants on the spiritual path are now ready to accept their own self-empowerment. When we all really understand the possibilities of our awesome power and abilities, our beliefs about ourselves will expand. Very often our guides and angels will present scenarios to us in order to empower us and encourage us to step into our higher roles. The base chakra assists by offering memories or prompts from previous incarnations that show us in a higher light. Any memories that do not serve are left behind.

Visualization to Anchor and Expand the Higher Base Chakra

1. Prepare for meditation. Create a sacred space and ensure that you are undisturbed.
2. Light a candle and dedicate it to yourself and your mighty power.
3. Call upon the Cosmic Diamond Violet Flame to wash through your four-body system, leaving it purified and clear. Also bring this flame through your 12 chakras.
4. Ask Archangels Gabriel and Zadkiel to place you within a shining cosmic diamond for the remainder of this meditation.
5. Sit quietly as they do this for you. See and feel this diamond shimmering around you, flowing with higher facets of the Violet Flame.
6. Bring your attention to your base chakra. Move into it. What colour do you perceive?
7. If there are any traces of red, move them with gentle hand movements into your cosmic diamond.
8. See the energy transmuted instantly into higher light.
9. Ask Archangel Gabriel to bring forth the highest facet of platinum light and fill your base chakra with this ray.
10. See it swirling and gleaming with this radiant energy.
11. As your fifth-dimensional base chakra anchors permanently and expands, invoke your monadic presence to anchor its higher energies into your base via your Antakarana bridge.

12. Feel a column of higher light moving down through the top of your head to merge with the platinum of your base.
13. At this point, sense and allow all the amazing achievements of mastery that you have ever experienced to flow into you and light you up.
14. Flood this energy from your base into your entire four-body system and allow it also to illuminate your merkabah.
15. Take a few moments to sense the energies of your base. When you are ready, stand on your feet.
16. Facing a mirror, look yourself in the eyes and say out loud:
17. 'I AM an ascended master. I AM, I AM, I AM.'
18. Repeat this three times, or as often as you wish.
19. Thank Archangels Gabriel and Zadkiel and the dragons.
20. Open your eyes, smile and take your mastery out into the world.

CHAPTER 8

The Expanded Sacral Chakra

The fifth-dimensional sacral chakra has provided some challenging lessons to those on the ascension pathway. This chakra is concerned with our sexuality and interrelating with others. Family relationships tend to be formed from this chakra, depending on the karmic blueprint that our soul brings into incarnation.

In the Golden Era of Atlantis the people sometimes took an androgynous form, as they had transcended the sacral lessons. They would only express their sexuality if they wanted to bring in a new soul. The energy of this chakra was expressed as pure love.

When Atlantis fell, the higher connection between souls was replaced by behaviour that bonded people only on a physical level. Those lessons have now been learned, but the residual patterns are ingrained in many people, who are still acting them out, oblivious of the changes around them.

Because the fifth-dimensional chakra column has been anchoring in high-frequency individuals, it has highlighted the clearance needed in the sacral centres. When this happens, souls are presented with relationship challenges that require great wisdom, discernment and trust in the intuition. When you pass these final tests, you step into a glorious fifth-dimensional vibration.

Those who have attained this level of sacral light attract souls who allow them the freedom to be themselves. This means they can express their true light. A yearning to connect with their divine complement has added a higher dynamic to spiritual relationships.

At the Harmonic Convergence in 1987, the Aquamarine Ray embraced Earth again, flooding it with the energies of love and feminine compassion. A trine of great beings, the Angel Mary, Mother Mary and Isis, are holding this luminous healing ray. They have been directing this higher light to enter the sacral chakras of receptive souls and be distributed throughout the four-body system. This means that humanity can start to experience true love again.

Spiritual mastery requires full control over every situation that is presented. The higher forces designed many scenarios to test seekers and raise their levels of discernment. During the transition to a higher frequency, it can be quite difficult to distinguish between the energies of the heart and the sacral. When you attract a relationship via the third-dimensional sacral chakra, it usually implies a physical connection only. The fifth seeks transcendent love. However, a deeper soul connection is found within the heart.

As your sacral chakra starts to develop and grow, a remarkable expansion takes place. A soft luminous pink light of pure love glows there and then spreads to all who are near you. Your sacral chakra then expands and fills the entire hip area.

Every soul who masters the lessons of the sacral chakra adds to the wave of change that is lighting up planet Earth. This enables the souls who follow to have an easier passage through their tests and initiations.

As the sacral chakra continues its rapid expansion, the higher energy of transcendent love that is held there draws partners together. A sacral that matches the vibration of someone else's will unify the two souls in perfect harmony. It is important, though, that the souls have lessons to learn from each other and that they learn in a manner that will assist their pathways. This will happen as we learn to follow the guidance of the higher energies bringing us together.

When family members connect through their higher sacral chakras, karmic bonds dissolve. This means that all the individuals within the family can be independent and free to enjoy relationships based on love and mutual respect.

When all our sacral chakras are fifth-dimensional, they will bring joy, light and unconditional love into all our relationships on Earth.

Visualization to Expand the Sacral Chakra

1. Prepare for meditation. Relax and ensure that you will be undisturbed in your sacred space.
2. Light a candle and dedicate it to the mighty fire dragons. Invoke them to join you.
3. Ask them to clear your physical, mental, emotional and spiritual bodies of anything that you wish to release. Be very specific.
4. See and feel them illuminating and burning your stuff.
5. Ask them now to start to focus on your chakras and work from the Stellar Gateway down to the Earth Star.
6. When they reach the sacral, call upon Archangel Gabriel to join them.
7. Ask Archangel Gabriel to place an expanding diamond within your sacral as the dragons continue with their work.

8. Focus on this diamond. See its bright facets absorbing all you wish to transcend.
9. See also any physical relationships that you may have had being drawn into the diamond. The diamond may also contain souls from past lives who still carry personal karma with you.
10. When this diamond is as full as you can make it, ask the dragons to remove it and take it away for deep processing.
11. In your mind's eye explore your sacral. How does it feel? How bright is the pink light radiating from it? How large is it? Has it expanded?
12. Invite Archangel Gabriel to continue working with this chakra for you for two further days under the Ray of Grace.
13. Invite your soul family to start connecting with you to fill your life with meaningful fifth-dimensional relationships.
14. Thank the fire dragons and Archangel Gabriel for their help.
15. Open your eyes and be ready to draw souls filled with love to you.

CHAPTER 9

The Expanded Navel Chakra

Our navel chakra works to unify our energies with those of all other forms of life. When it is in place, awake and spinning, we are fully aware of our infinite connection to the universe.

As the higher ascension energies continue to flood the Earth, they are bringing this chakra into operation. This will assist us to come together in communities of unconditional love. People will learn to co-operate for the highest good and see the best in one another. Cultures will respect and honour their differences.

Archangel Gabriel assists with the development of the navel chakra, and when it spins at a fifth-dimensional frequency, we start to experience lessons that pertain to our divine mission. Our soul families are drawn to us at this time and a spiritual support network forms around us to guide us onto the golden pathway. These events have been orchestrated to flow simultaneously and very quickly. We now have the additional benefits of social media to connect us to like-minded people around the world, and this enables us to share our knowledge and understandings with others on a daily basis.

The navel chakra allows us to experience true perception and Oneness. When we are aware of our true essence, we see the world around us with enlightened vision.

Our universal connection to other souls is so powerful that many people are now waking up and are taking immediate action to bring balance to Earth. Examples of the navel chakra working can be seen everywhere, as the higher forces create events that invoke a sense of community in the hearts of the masses. Even some challenging circumstances are allowing people to meet and communicate with a sense of togetherness.

When we focus on the connections that our navel chakra reveals to us, we can begin to understand the deeper layers of our existence. It connects us to the vast energies of the universe and we can link in to the higher dimensions. These are filled with the illuminated souls who have guided us since our journey first began. As we fully accept our infinite bond to them, their energy is drawn to us. We then begin to embody Christ Light in all that we think and do.

This process is one of the most powerful that we can experience. It enables us to embrace every soul as our brother or sister, regardless of where they are or what they are doing.

The people of Golden Atlantis were able to experience the power of the navel chakra fully and live in a state of Oneness with each other. They knew the ground they walked on was a conscious entity, so they honoured it. They loved the birds because they knew they were the messengers of the angels. They worshipped the stars because they knew that they were flooding them with higher light. Every soul they met was seen as a brother or a sister, regardless of their genetic connection to them. Their ability to embrace others was their key to achieving the higher aspects of physical ascension on Earth. Their lives were filled with love and beauty on a daily basis.

Every experience of unity that they had was recorded in the blueprint of their navel chakras. As we now remember how our higher chakras work, we can access the memories that are stored here. The next phase of our ascension process is being orchestrated to unify our societies once again, but there is still much work to do before we can achieve this.

As we start to work on a deeper level with our navel chakras, we will see them begin to glow with golden light. This begins as a small dot in the centre and spreads outwards as we expand into a state of higher consciousness. When we learn to accept everyone on Earth as a part of ourselves, we will experience the unity that existed in Golden Atlantis. Earth will move permanently into the fifth dimension and we will live as One with Source.

Visualization to Expand the Navel Chakra

1. Prepare for meditation. Relax in your favourite sacred space and light a candle.
2. Call upon the mighty solar fire dragons to purify you and your space to the highest level possible.
3. See and feel these beautiful golden dragons swirling from the core of the Great Central Sun to be with you.
4. Visualize them moving around you clockwise and anti-clockwise in a vortex of golden fire.
5. Ask them to remove anything that is keeping you separated from others on your pathway. This may be experiences that you have had in this lifetime or many others.
6. Sense and feel the ninth-dimensional fire opening you up to all sentient beings.
7. When you feel pure and clear, thank the dragons for their work.
8. Call to the mighty Archangel Gabriel. Ask him to light up your navel chakra at its highest frequency.

9. Your navel chakra sits between your solar plexus and sacral. See it glowing like your own personal Sun.
10. Visualize golden-orange threads of pure light flowing out and connecting you to every single living thing on this planet – the birds, animals, insects, people, plants and trees.
11. Feel this connection also spreading to all non-sentient life-forms – the rocks, crystals and mountains of Earth. Feel their vibration as an intimate part of you.
12. Take this connection higher now and see your filaments of light moving up through time and space to join with other universes. Acknowledge the souls that live there and allow their knowledge and peace to flow through you.
13. Ask your navel chakra to send a message of peace and unity to everyone on Earth.
14. See your navel chakra sending this message through golden threads that connect you to these souls.
15. Focus on your navel chakra expanding until it encompasses the width of your body and is glowing with the brightest light.
16. Open your eyes, and know that you are One with All That Is.

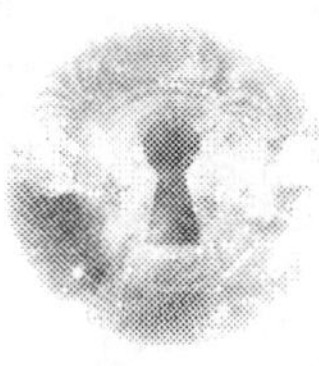

CHAPTER 10

The Expanded Solar Plexus Chakra

The solar plexus is an incredibly powerful psychic centre. It holds our gut feelings and sends out feelers to check what is happening around us. For thousands of years the souls on Earth ignored the psychic ability of this chakra and used their logical minds to navigate their pathways.

At the Harmonic Convergence in 1987, the Intergalactic Council decreed it was time for the higher solar plexus to anchor. They returned tools such as the Violet Flame of Transmutation to Earth to enable us to disperse the old and replace it with higher possibilities. So St Germain organized a massive clearance operation using the Violet Flame. Many karmic and energetic agreements are held in the solar plexus chakra and these were released at or after the Cosmic Moment in 2012. When it is fifth-dimensional, your solar plexus glows bright gold.

Under the guidance of the Intergalactic Council, the lightworkers of the first ascension wave, in an act of unconditional love, agreed to support others with the light of their fifth-dimensional solar plexus. The lightworkers passed through their own solar plexus chakras the energies of those who had lost their way. They then transmuted the old. This lifted the overall vibration of many who unconsciously wanted to join the second ascension wave and allowed them to see life from a higher perspective. They could then take any opportunity to evolve that was offered to them.

This has been a challenging mission for the lightworkers, who have been dealing with their own energies as well as assisting those around them. Some lightworkers have had to step back to recover their light and spiritual equilibrium.

The higher realms are now assisting with this mission and recently cords and attachments from millions of solar plexus chakras were cleared with downloads of cosmic light. This has been a great relief for the lightworkers on Earth, as they no longer have to manage the energies of others unless they choose to do so. Their rewards of this work are an advanced and powerful fifth-dimensional solar plexus chakra that glows with Christ Light. This chakra can now send out huge waves of energy into the world and assess what is happening around them. Its power is so vast that it has the ability to reach through multiple dimensional spaces at once. This allows us all to feel the energies of places or situations clearly and then discern the correct course of action.

To further speed up this process, many souls on the ascension path have taken physical action to free themselves or otherwise change their circumstances and follow their true calling.

The solar plexus is also guiding us by bringing to our conscious awareness deeper changes that need to be made. These decisions are usually life-changing and are drawn to our attention by strong prompts from our souls via our gut feelings.

The Golden Age now requires all of us on the master pathway to be fully responsible for our own energies. We must also be aware of the impact that our energy fields have on those around us. When your solar plexus chakra glows with bright golden light, it is free from the influence of others and indicates a higher state of mastery.

Visualization to Expand the Solar Plexus Chakra

1. Prepare for meditation. Light a candle and relax where you will be undisturbed.
2. Focus on your breathing and still your mind with deep, slow in-breaths.
3. On every out-breath, imagine your solar plexus glowing brightly with pure golden light.
4. Focus on your chakra and go within it. Feel its glowing energy.
5. How is it serving you? Is it clear and free?
6. Call upon the mighty fire dragons to join you in your meditation. Feel their radiant energy swirling around you, lighting up your sacred space.
7. Ask them to cleanse and purify any energy that exists within your solar plexus that does not belong to you.
8. Relax and feel their ascended fire cleansing these energies. You are pure, bright and clear.
9. View your solar plexus now. See how it is glowing.
10. Send a feeler of energy from your solar plexus into the seventh dimension. Push this light out from where you are sitting and see it enter a higher space.
11. Ask your solar plexus to record what it sees and bring impressions back to you in a form that you can easily understand.
12. Take the first thing that is given to you and write it down if you wish.
13. Call on Archangel Uriel to work with you for seven days to expand your solar plexus chakra to its maximum potential.
14. Thank the fire dragons and Archangel Uriel for their help.
15. Open your eyes and glow with the confidence of an enlightened master.

Decree to Release All Past-Life Cords and Contracts

Invite the mighty fire dragons to assist you.

Then, facing the East at sunrise, say this decree aloud three times to the universe:

> *'I, [name], in the name of God, under the Law of One, completely rescind any past-life or current agreements or contracts that I have made in the physical or etheric world.*
>
> *As a master, I now dissolve all energy vows.*
>
> *I command the complete freedom of my bodies and soul to complete my mission here on Earth.*
>
> *I now illuminate my chakras to their maximum potential and dedicate myself in service to Source.*
>
> *I AM a master in all that I AM.'*

When you have completed this, finish with 'It is so' and feel the words being taken to Source by the fire dragons. Remember to thank them.

Visualize your solar plexus chakra glowing with golden light as you take complete charge of your master pathway.

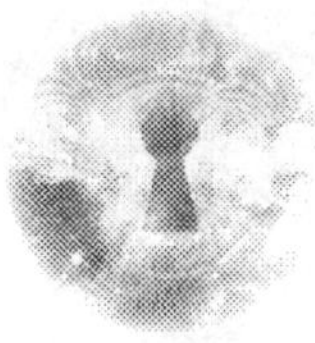

CHAPTER 11

The Expanded Heart Centre

Everyone on Earth now has the opportunity to work with their fifth-dimensional ascension chakras. A large rise in vibration occurred on the Summer Solstice 2014. The concentration of light enabled a window of energy to open on Earth and took another few million souls over the ascension threshold.

The fifth-dimensional column of chakras becomes operational when we reach a light percentage of at least 79 per cent. The physical body and the subtle bodies all have to rise in harmony together, and this is when our ascension truly begins.

Many people on Earth have now achieved this level. They are working their way through their tests and lessons and starting to use their expanded light bodies.

The heart centre is the core of the ascension process. It begins the illumination of the four-body system by connecting to the Cosmic Heart and flooding us with Christ consciousness. This is the start of enlightenment, for it enables us to experience life from a higher perspective.

Walking mastery was in operation in the era of Golden Atlantis and has recently been reinstated as an agreement between the people on Earth and the Intergalactic Council. This new agreement enables us to hold very high quantities of light and stay in a physical body. It is known as an Adam Kadmon blueprint, in which the 12 fifth-dimensional chakras are fully operational and the 24 strands of DNA are active – 12 strands pertaining to the physical body and 12 to the spiritual body.

The fifth-dimensional heart centre shines with a pure white vibration and contains 33 chambers of unconditional love. As we climb the ladder of ascension, our hearts start to shine with the higher Christed Ray frequencies and glow with a beautiful golden-white light.

Our heart chakras also become much larger. The centres of advanced souls extend from shoulder to shoulder to allow a high flow of frequencies and have the ability to pass light to other people. This enables us to send love to others without having to speak.

The heart chakra of a master is also capable of awakening mastery in others. For example, if you leave your house in the morning with a fifth-dimensional frequency, the codes of mastery are passed to everyone you meet. A room full of people can become fifth-dimensional when you are near them.

Every chakra has a memory or energetic blueprint and this is very similar to the muscle memory of an athlete. Once the chakras pick up the higher vibration, they immediately wake up and shine with their higher potential. This is helping the ascension process move with incredible speed.

The Intergalactic Council have said that millions of illuminated hearts are now shining on Earth and more are awakening every second.

The huge influx of divine feminine energy now flowing into the planet is spiritualizing the masculine and balancing it. This allows everything to be seen from an angelic perspective and is one of the first signs that a soul has woken up and is starting to work with Christ consciousness energy. Those in power will eventually be aware of this viewpoint. Then our societies will become full of light and love.

The fifth-dimensional heart chakra is also the centre of deep personal truth. Jesus Christ ascended on Earth by speaking his heartfelt truth in the face of adversity. His heart was so pure that it opened a higher-dimensional space on this planet to allow the Christ Light to return.

All masters on the ascension pathway are now being tested on the strength in their hearts. The lessons we take may not be as difficult as those Jesus experienced, because his job was to make this process easier for those who came after him to Earth.

One of the blessings we are receiving during this 20-year transition period on Earth is a download of the Christ Light. Every single soul on Earth is now being deluged with these frequencies from the centre of the Cosmic Heart through the Moon.

In addition the facets of the higher heart are now starting to accept the light codes of Christ Light flowing in from the Lyran stargate. Archangel Christiel opened this portal in preparation for the second wave of the ascension process, which is now fully underway.

Visualization to Activate the Fifth-Dimensional Heart Chakra

1. Relax and prepare for meditation. Light a candle and find a sacred space.
2. Sit quietly and focus upon your breathing.
3. Feel your breath filling your lungs, and as you breathe out see it as golden-white light.
4. Bring your attention to the centre of your chest. See your heart centre as pure radiant white surrounded by a beautiful golden glow.

5. With each in-breath, see your heart expanding until it has reached the width of your shoulders.
6. Feel its power and magnificence and see it connected to the higher realms by golden threads of light.
7. Ask your heart a question. This can be anything that currently concerns you about yourself or our planet.
8. Wait for its response. It may come in the form of a picture, words or feelings.
9. Take the first answer that is given to you. Thank your heart.
10. Now think of family, friends or even souls who are not close to you physically.
11. See them cocooned in the centre of your glowing heart, bathed in its radiance and light.
12. See their hearts starting to glow like yours.
13. Ask Archangels Chamuel, Christiel and Mary to illuminate all the facets of your heart during the day and night.
14. Ask them to take your light and spread it to your soul family.
15. Open your eyes and be ready to spread your light to all you meet.

CHAPTER 12

The Expanded Throat Chakra

The power of the spoken word is incredible. Within the essence of every word there are multiple layers of codes and vibrations. These affect everything around them. This has been recognized for millennia and people have been very careful about the vibrations they have distributed from this very commanding chakra.

Because people usually communicated by telepathy during the Golden Era of Atlantis, vocal communication and language were rudimentary. However, the people considered that the voices of their brothers and sisters were very sacred. They honoured every sound that was uttered and they only spoke loving, positive words. In fact there were no other words in their vocabulary. They lived in the now and only had a present tense. The voice is a sound box that massages a person internally, and this affirmative vocal melody enabled the inhabitants of Atlantis to maintain inner harmony. This was then reflected externally and kept their auras and fields completely clear. Discussions would be settled by agreeing on what was for the highest good, for everyone wanted to be fair and honest. They would apply the Violet Flame and higher gem rays to cleanse their fields. They also exercised great will and self-control at all times.

Their throat chakras became so powerful that the sound of their voices was used to provide healing in the temples. The sonic vibrations could harmonize the four-body system in a matter of seconds.

But in the final days of Atlantis, the people no longer listened to the wisdom of the High Priests and Priestesses. Because of this, the priesthood protected their sacred knowledge by downloading it into specially prepared very high-frequency quartz crystals. Sacred knowledge from the 12 temples was stored in crystal skulls, one for each area of Atlantis. This information was then transferred into a 13th skull, the amethyst one that is safely hidden on the inner planes. When enough people are living in the fifth dimension as enlightened masters, this will all be returned to us.

Archangel Michael oversees the development of the fifth-dimensional throat chakra. His role is vital. He frees this centre of all cords to allow the light to flow unhindered. When the higher chakra is ready to descend into the column, he merges his energy with the throat area. This clears and prepares it and allows this glorious centre of truth and power to anchor permanently there.

The colour of the fifth-dimensional throat chakra is an electric royal blue. As the chakra rises in frequency, a diamond spectrum of light becomes visible. This is a reflection of the heart of the master. In the upper ranges of the fifth dimension, the diamond light radiates out so strongly that it pierces all dimensional veils, allowing us to communicate directly with higher beings.

The Illumined Beings who are here to assist us take advantage whenever possible of this opportunity to speak with people on Earth. Some souls find themselves channelling the ancient languages of light from the higher learning planes. They speak in vibrations that are recognized by the energy bodies before the sound is transformed into healing. When this occurs, great accelerations take place in those who hear them, as dormant light codes are activated in their soul blueprints.

Beings who communicate physically with Earth through sound vibrations are usually Sirian or Pleiadean, as these beings have been working closely with the masters of Earth since Lemurian times. Commander Ashtar is a Venusian avatar who regularly releases information from his Intergalactic Fleet to those who are capable of accepting or transmitting the frequency through their throat chakra.

One of the greatest joys of life as an ascended master is experiencing the freedom to speak your truth with purity of heart. Pure words bring unconditional love into the lives of all who hear them. You automatically trust someone whose throat chakra is vibrating with truth.

As Earth progresses into the fifth dimension, everyone on Earth will be required to speak the truth of their soul. When all members of the human race have fully connected with one another on a conscious level, there will be no need for secrets, as all will be revealed through the vibration of their auras and fields. Pure truth will shine from the Earth, which will radiate golden light once again.

Visualization to Clear and Expand the Throat Chakra

1. Prepare for meditation. Find a quiet sacred place where you will be undisturbed and light a candle if you wish.
2. Hold a favourite crystal. Clear quartz would be perfect for this exercise.
3. Invoke the mighty Archangel Michael and ask him to be your guide and companion during this visualization.
4. Ask him to place his hand upon your throat, lighting up your chakra so that it is the brightest royal blue.

5. Holding your crystal in your right hand, place it upon your throat.
6. Sense and feel the energy amplifying and anchoring your energy into the fifth-dimensional frequency.
7. Tune into your throat chakra. Are there any blockages in there? Allow Archangel Michael's energy to release and dissolve any energies that prevent you from speaking your spiritual truth.
8. Now invoke the presence of Archangel Gabriel. See him holding a sparkling rainbow diamond in his hands.
9. Invite him to place the diamond in your throat. Sense and feel the vibration of your chakra rising further still.
10. See light codes and pure vibrations reaching out from your throat and connecting to luminous beings from higher dimensions. Do you have any questions for them?
11. If so, sit quietly and await your response. This can arrive in any form, so be open and ready to receive.
12. Thank Archangels Michael and Gabriel for their help.
13. Open your eyes and smile. Know that every word you speak will be infused with pure love and will open the hearts of those around you.

CHAPTER 13

The Expanded Third Eye Chakra

Walking mastery requires individuals to be completely self-sufficient on their soul path, taking full responsibility for their lives, taking their own decisions and standing in their personal power. At last, souls are now reconnecting with their true selves and stepping into full mastery.

One of the most effective tools that we have on Earth is the ability to create our own reality. We are now learning to do this in a positive manner, with the assistance of the higher realms. When our planet started to rise in frequency, we gained access to our master abilities again and started to remember how to use them effectively. The 20-year period of transition to the fifth dimension is being used to teach us once more to create the life that brings us soul satisfaction.

In recent times the fifth-dimensional crown chakra has started to merge with the crystal ball of the third eye. This is giving lightworkers a huge increase in their manifestation abilities, and these skills are supported by the rise in planetary energies. Since the Cosmic Moment, the fifth-dimensional energy on Earth has become very accessible. This is now allowing us to see how quickly our thoughts turn into reality. As a result, new scenarios are challenging us to manifest from a pure heart. We are reminded to focus on what we really want the universe to deliver for the highest good.

The merging of our third eye and crown centre is a natural progression for our fifth-dimensional chakras and requires precision handling. Our third eyes are now expanding, so that more and more of us are seeing the world of spirit. Furthermore, the fifth-dimensional third eye allows us to enjoy clairvoyance, clairaudience, clairsentience and claircognizance. Our abilities are expanding rapidly.

The fifth-dimensional third eye looks like a pure crystal ball that glows with an emerald light. This is often amplified by the energies of Archangel Raphael, who is responsible for the development with this chakra.

As we start to anchor and use the expanded third eye, it begins to unify with the crown chakra and a new energy screen starts to form on the outside of our head. This is usually found 15cm (6in) in front of the forehead and resembles a golden-green screen onto which we project our thoughts and wishes for manifestation. When we begin to access these abilities, we are co-creating with the Divine at a very high level.

During Golden Atlantis these abilities were honed to perfection by the Alta-Magi. These highly evolved beings worked with the priesthood of Atlantis as masters of manifestation. They were so well trained that they could create solid objects with the power of their minds. Many of us are now remembering our Atlantean lifetimes and are stepping forwards to carve a path of light directly into the fifth dimension.

The higher energies are allowing us the freedom to create love and beauty in many different ways. As masters, we are responsible for teaching ourselves and others how to do this. One of the fastest ways that we can achieve higher manifestation with the third eye is by training ourselves to live lightly and think positively at all times. This takes practice and dedication, but when we do achieve it, we can enjoy our creations of love and bliss.

There are two mighty ascended masters who are now helping us to blend our third eye and crown chakras. These are Lord Voosloo and the Master Serapis Bey, who were both High Priests in the Golden Age of Atlantis. They initiated and trained specifically chosen high-frequency Magi to access incredible powers that could manipulate reality.

During the Golden Era of Atlantis, the Magi were at the forefront of any work that was being done to raise the frequency of the Atlantean continent.

Visualization to Merge the Crown and Third Eye Chakras with Lord Voosloo and Serapis Bey

1. Prepare for meditation. Ensure that you eat lightly during the day and drink plenty of fluid.
2. Call forth the dragons of the Cosmic Diamond Violet Flame to purify your physical, mental, emotional and spiritual bodies.
3. Feel and see these powerful elementals lighting up every cell of your being with crystal violet fire.
4. When you are sparkling and clear, ask Lords Voosloo and Serapis Bey to come to you.
5. They join you. Serapis Bey is dressed in pure white, and Voosloo is wearing robes that glow like the Sun.
6. They are leading you down beautiful candlelit steps into a circular room. This room is adorned with golden symbols on the walls and goblets of golden fire that blaze with a pure etheric light.
7. You are invited to sit on an ornate seat in the centre of this room and close your eyes. Feel yourself being illuminated by the pure golden fire that ignites every cell of your body at a fifth-dimensional frequency.

8. Become aware of your 12 chakras lighting up in harmony with this light.
9. Lords Voosloo and Serapis Bey stand in front of you. You see that you are also surrounded by a circle of gentle and powerful beings. These are the priests and priestesses of Golden Atlantis.
10. Lord Voosloo places his hand upon your crown chakra. Sense and feel his energy pulsing through your aura and fields.
11. Visualize your third eye glowing crystal emerald green and mixing with the pure gold of your crown.
12. Energy is spreading down through your body and forming a beautiful golden-green cloak around your body and your fields. Relax and breathe deeply as this energy integrates with you.
13. Serapis Bey now places a handful of his White Ascension Flame into each of your chakras.
14. Feel the flame illuminating your Stellar Gateway, soul star, causal, crown, third eye, throat, heart, solar plexus, navel, sacral, base and Earth Star chakras.
15. As this is completed, Serapis Bey speaks. He tells you that you have been gifted and graced with an amazing responsibility for your awakening planet.
16. Now your abilities to create your new reality will be enhanced. You will be able to manifest love and beauty around you with the speed of an ascended master.
17. Use this gift to co-create pure love in your life and the lives of others.
18. Take a moment to visualize this golden-green cloak around you and see its light flowing from your third eye to everything that you focus upon.
19. Stand and thank Serapis Bey, Lord Voosloo and the Atlantean souls who have joined you for this ceremony.
20. When you are ready, leave the beautiful room and walk back up the steps to your reality.
21. Breathe deeply and open your eyes. Be ready to create with the divine power of an ascended master.

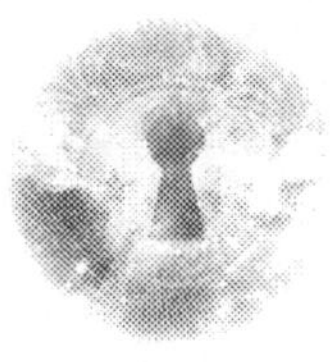

CHAPTER 14

The Expanded Crown Chakra

The role of our crown chakra has changed dramatically as we have embraced the higher ascension energies. Each of the thousand petals of the crown is now like a radio antenna looking for higher frequencies it can tune into. It will then bring these ascended vibrations into our pineal gland.

As the crown rises in frequency, all seventh to ninth-dimensional frequencies are rerouted to the Stellar Gateway chakra, which becomes a chalice linked to the Great Central Sun. A multitude of light codes spanning the universes will pour into this golden chalice. Depending on your mission, your Stellar Gateway will be tuned to specific codes that support your soul energy. Guided by your monad, your individual cosmic and universal links can then be activated for your ascension process.

Archangel Jophiel is responsible for assisting us with the early stages of the development of the fifth-dimensional crown, and he gently fills this chakra with higher vibrations to help it to expand. As this occurs, we also receive a wave of energy from our monadic presence. This download of light spreads from our crown centre through our spiritual fields, which extend around us for up to 32km (20 miles). Our spiritual fields contain the many dormant light codes that we have chosen for our mission on Earth. These codes are now being activated, guided by the higher realms.

The crown chakra then starts to receive energy and instructions directly from our soul blueprint and this helps to guide us onto our master pathway. The experiences that we receive during this process are both challenging and expansive.

Our ascension mission is very specific. We have incarnated on Earth at this time with important jobs to do and it is essential that we focus directly on the task in hand. As our crown chakra becomes fifth-dimensional, it draws our attention to inner knowledge and guidance. During the last paradigm on Earth, many spiritual souls followed the promptings of their guides and angels, but these are now stepping back to allow us to become self-sufficient.

While Tim was writing the first Archangel guide book with Diana, he experienced this for himself. He had always been in touch with his angels and had become very used to the continual flow of higher information. But while he was writing *The Archangel Guide to Ascension*, his flow of information stopped. Naturally, this disturbed him, as he had never experienced this before. He took some time out to meditate on the problem and tuned into the guidance of his heart for the solution.

After a short while, the issue became clear. The vibration on Earth was rising sharply and had created a huge change in his energy fields. He then started to look internally for the knowledge that was needed to complete the book and found that his library of information from Atlantis had been activated. He was able to use his knowledge as a High Priest to complete the book and to access vital information that he had stored away many lifetimes ago in Golden Atlantis.

Throughout that year he saw many others experiencing this situation and responding to it in the same way. This was confirmation that our responsibilities as masters have begun to increase and grow.

Throughout history many Illumined Masters have been portrayed with halos, indicating that light or knowledge is pouring from their crown chakras. As the fifth-dimensional energies expand within us, our crown begins to glow with golden light and the thousand petals of higher consciousness open to create a perfect balance of enlightened wisdom.

We have often had many lifetimes as masters and we all have the opportunity to access this wisdom now to help Earth move into the Golden Age of Gaia.

Visualization to Expand the Crown Chakra and Unlock Your Master Wisdom

1. Prepare for meditation. Eat lightly throughout the day and drink plenty of pure water.
2. Relax within your sacred space. Light a candle if you wish and place crystals around you.
3. Call upon the mighty fire dragons to clear your chakras and four-body system of any dense energies.
4. Relax as they swirl around you, lighting you up with their golden flames.
5. Call on Lord Serapis Bey and ask him to place the White Ascension Flame of Atlantis into your 12-chakra system.
6. See him approach you dressed in pure white. He is smiling and holding the White Ascension Flame in his hands.
7. Feel your chakras lighting up from your Stellar Gateway down to your Earth Star. Relax and allow this energy to flood through you until you are glowing and fifth-dimensional.
8. Serapis Bey is now inviting you to go with him to his pyramid in Hollow Earth. Together you walk along a tunnel of gold that is leading directly to his Golden Crystal Pyramid, his Pyramid of Agartha.

9. He invites you to stand at the doorway to his pyramid. When you knock, the door swings open and you walk into a beautiful room with a golden throne in the centre.
10. Serapis Bey invites you to be seated on this golden throne and focus on your crown chakra. Feel it glowing bright gold and starting to open like a thousand-petalled lotus.
11. Serapis Bey now hands you a large and ancient book and you place it on your lap.
12. He tells you that this book contains your wisdom from all of your lifetimes as a master. He invites you to open it.
13. As you open the book, beautiful shapes, codes and golden letters rise off the pages and start to enter your crown chakra.
14. Feel them starting to open your crown to its maximum capacity as the codes start to flow throughout your body and energy fields.
15. Relax and breathe deeply as this process lights you up with ancient wisdom, light and knowledge.
16. Serapis Bey is stroking these codes and letters into your aura and lighting them up so that they shine brightly. Take a few moments to observe this in your mind's eye. Do you recognize any of the symbols?
17. You are now glowing with ancient knowledge and light and you can access this wisdom for your higher ascension pathway.
18. Thank Serapis Bey and the fire dragons and leave his pyramid, knowing that you can return here anytime that you wish.
19. Open your eyes and smile. You are ready to bring your soul wisdom to others to help them on their journey.

CHAPTER 15

The Expanded Causal Chakra

The moon-white causal chakra is located just behind the rear of the skull. During Atlantean times it was as physical as the crown and occupied a space at the back of the skull, creating an elongated head. When it is first activated, it is separate from the head, resting between the crown and the soul star chakras. As the light level of a master rises, the causal unites with the fifth-dimensional chakra column. Then it is drawn into physical contact with the head.

The transcendent chakras are always fifth-dimensional. This is the third of the transcendent centres. It is connected to the Moon and is like your own personal Moon, absorbing and radiating divine feminine light. It acts as a magnet for lunar light, drawing it directly into the four-body system. This raises your vibration and illuminates the deep feminine wisdom held within your soul. Since the Cosmic Moment in 2012, the causal chakras of all awakened souls have expanded rapidly.

The divine feminine is one of the most powerful energies that has been cascading onto Earth in recent times. This vibration of wisdom and compassion was withdrawn at the fall of Atlantis and for the next 10,000 years its loss dramatically affected humanity's journey. However, it is returning to all of us now and is dissolving the unbalanced masculine force and allowing the heart to rule once more.

The Moon is playing a large and important role in this, for it is an ascended satellite that holds the higher aspects of the divine feminine. These are monitored and dispensed by the Universal Angel Mary and her team of unicorns. They harvest this pure and gentle feminine illumination at peak times and flood the people of Earth with waves of it to create softer possibilities.

The Moon also reflects the light of the Great Central Sun, known as Helios. This ninth-dimensional spiritual star sends light to Earth via our Sun. As this energy leaves Helios, it is divine masculine in vibration and balanced with the influence of Vesta, which is the divine feminine counterpart of the Central Sun system.

During full Moon periods on Earth, the powerful silver light pours into the minds of humanity and affects people profoundly, creating huge shifts in enlightenment in preparation for the pending new Golden Age.

Full Moons have always been times of magic and awe. It has long been recognized that animals and sensitive people can be profoundly affected by the vibrations they emit. Throughout 2014 and 2015 the full Moons became increasingly potent, culminating in the incredibly powerful full Moon of September 2015. Gaia herself has now received enough of the lunar light to balance the masculine and feminine energies on Earth. However, there will continue to be extraordinarily influential full Moons as the masculine and feminine energies of vast swathes of people come into equilibrium.

As well as absorbing and spreading the divine feminine light, the causal chakra has another powerful purpose: it provides the seeker with a deep and intimate connection to the world of spirit. The level of this connection depends on the psychic gifts an individual has brought forwards from their past lives. It is also contingent on their soul mission.

The causal also allows a two-way flow of energy and light from the angelic realms. This brings the angelic vibration to the individual and anchors it permanently. When the causal chakras of the lightworkers became active again, the unicorns connected their awesome pure light to Earth through these beings.

A unicorn will connect with you when it sees your light of service lighting up over your crown and will enter your energy fields through your causal chakra. This happening is so significant, beautiful and powerful that it has the potential to alter your soul path completely.

Unicorns are the only beings who carry pure grace as they work with Earth. They bless all circumstances with unconditional love. These mighty beings vibrate between the seventh and the ninth-dimensional frequency and of course the seventh-dimensional ones arrived first to help and illuminate us. In 2015, ninth-dimensional unicorns came in to light up and touch the hearts of everyone.

Archangel Christiel is in charge of the development of the causal chakra and because this chakra is so important in the progress of humanity's enlightenment, he continues to work with us all on our journey to become enlightened masters.

As the light held within all souls grows brighter, Archangel Christiel brings even higher aspects of Christ consciousness into Earth's energy field. This light shines through the causal chakra and the centre of the heart. The completion of this higher embodiment of Christ Light will occur before 2032 so that we are ready for the new Golden Age.

Visualization to Expand the Causal Chakra

1. Prepare for meditation. Pick a sacred spot and light a candle if you choose.
2. Call upon Archangel Christiel to fill your four-body system with ninth-dimensional Christ Light.
3. Breathe this into every cell of your body and allow it to wash you completely clean. Rest for a moment in this light.
4. Bring your attention to your causal chakra and see it glowing bright radiant white.
5. See it connecting to the Moon with pure white filaments reaching up to touch it.
6. Bring the light of the Moon back to your causal chakra and see it expanding until it completely merges with you.
7. Allow Archangel Christiel to anchor this higher aspect of the chakra into your physical body. Feel and sense how this affects your field of energy.
8. Sense your causal chakra sending out magnetic vibrations into the angelic realms.
9. Archangels and angels are now coming to you. They are carrying gifts of pure light in their hands. Behind them glides a magnificent ninth-dimensional unicorn.
10. Allow these beings to place their gifts within your causal chakra. Feel the beauty and light expanding your causal until it matches the luminosity of the Moon.
11. The unicorn approaches you now and she carries a message for your higher ascension pathway. This may come as words, sacred geometry or light codes.
12. Draw this into your heart centre and know that your journey will carry the brightest light.
13. Thank the angels and the unicorn and return to your sacred space.
14. Open your eyes and use your expanded causal to flood angelic light into the lives of everyone around you.

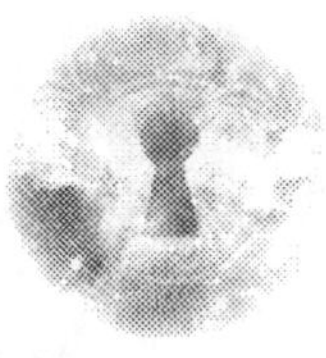

CHAPTER 16

The Expanded Soul Star

The soul star chakra is the second of the transcendent spiritual centres and it considerably influences our enlightenment. Located 30cm (12in) above the crown, immediately above the causal chakra in the integrated column, it is activated during the early stages of the ascension process. It is unique because it becomes accessible before a person reaches a 79 per cent light quotient. All that is required is for a soul to accept their spiritual mission.

The soul star chakra holds every single gift, talent and spiritual achievement that has been gained during a soul's journey. This includes knowledge and wisdom earned during lives that have been experienced in other bodies, dimensional spaces and universes. So once this chakra becomes active, a magnificent library of information becomes available to the seeker.

When the soul star first starts to wake, its development is overseen by Archangels Zadkiel and Mariel. These radiant beings are in continuous attendance during the early days of its activation. They ensure that it is opened and activated to its maximum capacity.

The soul star is divided into two aspects, higher and lower. The lower connects the soul with its essence, drawing in light from the monad to accelerate its chosen path. This occurred for many people while they were progressing into the fourth dimension. This is when your heart opens and you start to recognize your soul journey.

The higher aspect of your soul star is the true key to your wisdom as a master.

At the Summer Solstice of 2014, fifth-dimensional ascension chakras became available to everyone as the soul star moved into the next phase of its activation and its glorious bright magenta light anchored in millions of people. This opened doorways to past-life gifts, knowledge and consciousness.

With access to their treasure chest of cosmic and personal attainments, the enlightened masters of Earth are now starting to manifest great skills. This is moving everyone into a much higher vibration.

Tim had his first soul star experience in 2008. After a massive life change, he was visited by Archangel Michael during morning meditation. The archangel told him that although he loved him very much, he must now become more responsible for his own energies and not call on him so often.

Archangel Michael then presented Tim with a piece of ancient Atlantean technology called the Blue Star Seal that would allow him to manage his own energy systems. This was retrieved from Tim's soul star and activated. Tim's memories and gifts from his lifetime as Thoth then came flooding back. Five years later, Archangel Michael told him he could pass the technique to those who were ready for it, and he did so in *The Archangel Guide to Ascension*.

All seekers on the spiritual pathway have access to the same level of information. However each soul pathway is completely unique. The soul star chakra provides exactly what a master needs when they need it. It will never bring forwards information or memories that are not relevant or applicable at that time.

As you work directly with an expanded soul star, incredible doorways open. When you look directly into the soul star chakra you see lines of pure light moving through time and space. These lead via golden doors to memories of high-frequency lifetimes. These illuminated doorways are the etheric stores of knowledge connected to the monadic presence, Hollow Earth, the Halls of Amenti and the Akashic Records.

All these divine records are accessible, depending on your vibrational frequency. The more brightly you shine, the further your soul can travel to retrieve what you need. When you reach this level, Archangels Zadkiel and Mariel take a step back to allow you to stand in your own power. Many on the ascension path are now experiencing a withdrawal of spiritual assistance because of the clear light that they hold. The higher realms are observing us rather than leading us by the hand. Guidance is always available, but it is the masters of Earth who are really anchoring the light of the Aquarian Age.

During the Golden Era of Atlantis, the High Priests and Priestesses developed their own soul star chakras to their full potential. The Alta could use this chakra to develop spiritual tools which could raise the vibration of others. They could connect with the 12th-dimensional light of their own monads and this enabled them to access the blueprint for incredible technology. This was one of the factors that allowed Atlantis to become the foundation for fifth-dimensional life on Earth.

If you ever lived and worked in the Golden Era of Atlantis, you have the light and love of this time stored within your soul star chakras. It is this energy that will enable our planet to ascend gloriously over the next 20 years. Then we will start to progress to spiritual and technological heights that were not even imagined by the wise ones of Atlantis.

Visualization to Access the Soul Star Chakra

1. Prepare for meditation. Find a sacred space, light a candle if you choose and completely relax.
2. Close your eyes and breathe deeply. Bring your attention to your soul star chakra, 30cm (12in) above your head.
3. See it glowing an amazing luminous magenta. In the core is a bright blue light.
4. Focus on this blue light and move your energy into it. Feel it becoming one with you.
5. See yourself standing outside a glowing blue and magenta doorway. Archangels Zadkiel and Mariel are there to greet you.
6. They open the doorway for you and allow you to step in.
7. Before you is a shimmering silver pathway extending as far as the eye can see. There are glowing portals of light on each side of the path, each containing a gateway to a past life that you have lived.
8. These portals hold all your glorious spiritual achievements. Pick one and open it.
9. What energy is contained within it?
10. Take the first thing that is given to you and draw it into your heart centre. Feel the light from this lifetime raising your vibration to a new peak.
11. Pick another gateway. Ask Archangel Zadkiel and Mariel to assist you to open more doors if you wish.
12. Draw all the light into your heart and allow the codes and vibrations to expand throughout your body. Feel your personal cosmic knowledge lighting you up and making you glow.
13. Bring your attention back to your soul star chakra above your head. See how large and bright it has become.

14. Thank Archangels Zadkiel and Mariel and return to where you started.
15. Open your eyes and be ready to receive your ancient wisdom in whatever form it comes to you.

You can do this visualization as often as you wish.

CHAPTER 17

The Expanded Stellar Gateway

Viewed from the angelic realms, the illuminated Stellar Gateway chakra is the most magnificent sight. As our angels, guides and other beings of light observe our progress, they have the pleasure of watching our light body blossom with our soul essence. An incredibly bright light shines from our fifth-dimensional chakra column as it draws in the highest vibrations from all corners of the universe.

Every person's chakra system emits a unique light, for it radiates their individual soul mission for that lifetime. The task of the Stellar Gateway is to connect the individual soul in a physical body to the source of light from which they originate. This is the star or planet of origin.

When we had only seven operational chakras, our crown was in charge of receiving and processing all the inflow and information given to us. However, as we progress into the fifth-dimensional way of living, the Stellar Gateway takes this role. When it becomes active at the start of the ascension process, all our energy systems start to reroute their flow of light and power.

The Stellar Gateway has the ability to transcend all dimensional boundaries of time and space. Its job is to provide us with frequencies that extend way beyond our current physical capacity. It is capable of accepting light from a ninth-dimensional source and stepping it down to a level that is comfortable for us. Because of this amazing connection, many souls who are working with their fifth-dimensional chakra column are making spiritual progress more quickly than they anticipated.

The Stellar Gateway is a beautiful golden-orange colour when first anchored and activated and it is overseen by the Lord of Light, Archangel Metatron. He is the creator of all known light in our universe. During the early stages of our ascension journey he carefully pours light into this chakra to nurture our expansion. When the process is anchored, he stands back to allow us to expand at a rate that is in harmony with our soul mission.

The Stellar Gateway expands rapidly in the second stage of the ascension process. Many souls are currently at this level. The golden-orange colour takes on a brighter hue at this stage, as it is filled with the higher frequencies of Christ consciousness and the chakra constantly changes shape. Depending on our individual dynamism, it will form intricate sacred geometric shapes to magnetize the correct energies to the light body. These energies are always linked to the star or planetary system from which our soul originates. This ensures that the highest level of support is provided for us while we are on Earth.

Our soul may consciously send out requests for light and information and our Stellar Gateway will fulfil these. It also independently seeks out cosmic information for our soul growth. It is drawn to all sources of pure light in the vast reaches of space. This helps it to draw in new experiences for our learning process here on Earth.

When working like this, it forms a bright golden chalice with beautiful golden threads of light spreading from it up through the dimensions of time and space. This is why it is such an amazing spectacle to witness from the higher realms.

Since the Cosmic Moment in 2012, the Stellar Gateway has been responsible for receiving the first waves of light accessible to us from the Great Central Sun. This ninth-dimensional spiritual Sun is the source of light that feeds our own physical star.

Our Sun, which is clearly felt and seen here on Earth, has a much greater function than to provide us with light and heat. It physically steps down this ninth-dimensional light to a level with which the Earth can cope, acting as a transformer for the higher light codes as they are distributed constantly to us.

The Stellar Gateway is particularly linked to Mars and its ascended aspect, Nigellay. This planet or crescent radiates the light of the peaceful spiritual leader and its influence also helps to reflect and amplify the light.

In addition, our personal Stellar Gateway chakras are connected to the planetary Stellar Gateway chakra in the Arctic. This planetary portal rises in frequency to match the energy fields of Earth. When they rise in frequency, we do too. Only now are we truly seeing how deeply connected we really are to our planet.

During the Golden Era of Atlantis it was the advanced capabilities of the Stellar Gateway chakras that enabled the High Priests and Priestesses to communicate with the councils of other star systems. During deep meditation the Alta would consult with these beings of light, and as a result, the healing and advanced technologies of countless star beings were downloaded into their Stellar Gateways. They in turn passed it to the Magi for onward transmission to the temple priests, who lovingly turned it into physical information to help the people and advance their civilization to the higher fifth dimension.

During the entire period of Golden Atlantis, extraterrestrial and inter-dimensional civilizations came to visit Earth. Since that era, they have been sending their light and love to us here from their distant planes. They do this through the energy fields of those who are open and ready.

The blueprint of all this incredible knowledge is stored within the higher aspects of all Stellar Gateway chakras on Earth. It will be released when we are ready to utilize it again.

Visualization to Expand Your Stellar Gateway

1. Prepare for meditation. Find a sacred space and light a candle if you wish.
2. Relax and focus on your breathing.
3. Call on the ninth-dimensional Gold Ray of Christ to fill your four bodies and seal your sacred space. Breathe this energy into every cell of your being.
4. Bring your attention to your Stellar Gateway chakra 45cm (18in) above the top of your head.
5. See it glowing bright radiant gold and ask it to form a shape that reflects your soul essence.
6. Relax and allow your Stellar Gateway to take any shape that it wishes.
7. Ask it to call in the highest frequencies of light to you. These may come from any source in the universe, so be open to any information that may be presented.
8. See golden filaments of pure light spreading from your Stellar Gateway to connect with a source of higher light.
9. When you are connected, allow this light to flood down through the filaments into your chakra to expand it to the highest level possible.
10. Allow this light to flood down from your Stellar Gateway into the rest of your body and chakra system. See it moving down through your soul star, causal, crown, third eye, throat, heart, solar plexus, navel, sacral, base and finally your Earth Star.

11. Allow this light to ground via your Earth Star into the heart of Gaia and the planetary matrix.
12. Sense and feel the vibration of this gift to you and Mother Earth.
13. Be ready to start receiving higher levels of ascension information.
14. Open your eyes and glow with cosmic mastery.

Lord Kuthumi and the Halls of Learning

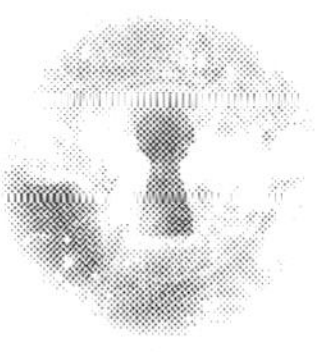

CHAPTER 18

Lord Kuthumi, World Teacher

Lord Kuthumi is one of the greatest Illumined Masters to have walked this planet. When you are on your ascension path to mastery and enlightenment, as you read or think about him, his energy touches you and expands your consciousness.

He is a Kumara, one of four souls who come from the heart of God and have special service work to do in the universe. When one of these four souls incarnates, it is born enlightened and illuminated.

Lord Kuthumi originates from Venus, the planet of love. During his long soul journey he has always demonstrated the power of love to all. He now vibrates on a crystal yellow ray, the colour of the illumined mind, and has just become the World Teacher. He has a history of remarkable and illustrious service to humanity, though this has been very challenging in many lifetimes.

His etheric retreat is above Agra, in India, over the beautiful Taj Mahal. In his lifetime as Shah Jahan, the Mogul Emperor, he experienced true love with his favourite wife, Mumtaz Mahal. When she died, he built the Taj Mahal as an offering of perfect love to her. This edifice was created with such adoration and attention to detail that it still radiates agape in its energy fields and draws those who are ready to experience unconditional and devotional love.

He also built the Red Fort in Delhi and the biggest mosque of the time in India and spent a considerable fortune on architectural projects. In addition he helped the poor and dispensed justice fairly. This was a very challenging lifetime for him, though, as his sons were in conflict. He lost much of his empire and one of his sons imprisoned him, so that he died in captivity. This lifetime strengthened him considerably on his path to mastery.

As St Francis of Assisi, he offered harmlessness and love to all creatures. His aura was so clear and calm that every animal who approached him felt totally safe and none would ever hurt him. That lifetime was not only about peace to all. As a monk with very determined ideas of service to God, he had to demonstrate considerable courage, trust and faith in his mission.

He also incarnated as John the Beloved, Balthazar, the wise man who divined the birthplace of Jesus, and Pharaoh Tutmoses III of Egypt.

For many years, Lord Kuthumi was the Chohan of the Second Ray, the Yellow Ray of Love and Wisdom. He has always been very interested in enlightening humanity about the spiritual laws. He was a founder member of the Knights Templar, who kept ancient esoteric secrets and protected pilgrims as they travelled on their quests. As Pythagoras, he introduced sacred geometry, numerology, mathematics and the incredible Music of the Spheres to the world and also formed a mystery school for the Great White Brotherhood. He is co-protector, with Archangel Michael, of the holy grail, which is the mystical quest for self-understanding and mastery.

As part of his selfless service, he is a hierarch of the Brotherhood of the Golden Robe, an order which spreads peace through golden light and takes on the burdens of the world. In addition, he is the doorkeeper of the ancient occult mysteries.

As World Teacher, he is now bringing esoteric information to those lightworkers who can understand it as our planet moves towards ascension. He radiates the crystalline quality of this high-frequency role.

His symbol has always been the six-pointed star, the symbol of Atlantis, of the merging of Heaven and Earth. However, it has now expanded so that six extra rays radiate out from it.

Before the Cosmic Moment in 2012 there were seven teaching schools in the etheric and Lord Kuthumi helped to run these with Dwjhal Khul. Since he has become World Teacher and Head of the Schools of Learning, he has created 12 schools on the inner planes in alignment with the rising energy and expectations of this universe. Beings attend these establishments not just from Earth but from all over the universes.

These are not primary schools, but an etheric university where those who wish to graduate as ascended masters of this universe are instructed via a series of courses. Many people think that you can only become an ascended master if you have a physical body. However, this is not so. Beings like Diana's guide Kumeka are Lords of Light and ascended masters, but have never incarnated on Earth. They have graduated through non-physical dimensions, learnings, tests, examinations and initiations.

There are a number of reasons for beings to remain in spiritual bodies. They may be deemed not ready for a physical experience, other spirits may need an Earth experience more, or a non-physical course may be more in alignment with their soul blueprint. In Diana's case, she and Kumeka are twin flames (*see page 246*) and their soul agreement is that she incarnates and he guides her from the inner planes. And so it has been for lifetimes.

Each of the 12 teaching 'buildings' of the etheric university is in circular form, like a pillared temple, and is glowing with radiant light. Students who are currently incarnate go there in their spirit bodies as they sleep.

The teaching methods are exactly the same as they were in the Golden Era of Atlantis. Each temple contains a crystal skull into which Lord Kuthumi downloads information and knowledge. There are also downloads from time to time from the Intergalactic Council. Serapis Bey, Dwjhal Khul, Lord Hilarion, Lord Voosloo and the Great Divine Director are among those who share their wisdom with the students of the universes.

Each student who applies and receives permission to enrol for these courses has their own individual crystal skull. They can link this to the main crystal skull in the temple to download group lessons. They then access the information by placing their skull on their third eye. They can also sign up for individually tailored lessons, which they access via the spiritual equivalent of a password. Many of those attending are helping Earth from non-physical dimensions.

Like Archangel Metatron's sub-temples, each of the teaching spaces in the Halls of Learning is bathed in an appropriate colour, and concrete information in the language of light is imparted in each one.

When you visit the World Teacher's educational temples, you receive great downloads of light containing the knowledge and wisdom that is perfect for your progress as a master. Enrolling in his teaching academy offers a fast-track programme to enlightenment and mastery.

Visualization to Enrol in Lord Kuthumi's Teaching Schools

1. Find a place where you can be quiet and undisturbed. Light a candle if possible.
2. Close your eyes and centre yourself by breathing comfortably.
3. Be aware of a crystal yellow light appearing in front of you. This forms a spiralling pathway into the inner planes.
4. As you follow the path, you look down and see the Taj Mahal below you, radiating glorious multi-coloured light.
5. A simple monk dressed in a brown habit is walking down the path to meet you. Birds and animals surround him and you recognize St Francis.
6. He welcomes and greets you warmly. Then he reminds you that the path to enlightenment and mastery may not always be easy, but it is always rewarding.
7. Ahead there is a huge luminous yellow-gold gate with a bell pull beside it. St Francis nods and smiles, so you pull the bell.
8. As the bell sounds, the gate swings open and Lord Kuthumi himself stands in front of you, his aura shimmering with light.
9. He smiles when he sees you.
10. You ask humbly for entry to his teaching school to accelerate your path to enlightenment and mastery.
11. Lord Kuthumi examines your aura and you have a sense of the colours around you swirling and shining.
12. He invites you to follow him into a lift that takes you to an elevated room.
13. As you look out of the window, you see 12 buildings streaming with various hues of coloured light.
14. Students of all shapes and sizes from all over the universes are milling in the central courtyard or entering the buildings. Their auras are

unbelievably bright and they glow with joy, dignity and a sense of soul satisfaction.

15. Lord Kuthumi asks you if you are ready to join his school.
16. If you wish to do so, you raise your hand and say solemnly:

    'I, [name], do apply to study in Lord Kuthumi's schools of light. I promise to do my best and honour the sacred spiritual teachings.'

17. Lord Kuthumi hands you a small crystal skull, which you take and hold carefully.
18. He says:

    'I accept you, [name], as a student in my schools of light. You are welcome.'

19. He indicates that it is time for you to leave and you enter the lift that takes you down to the main gate.
20. St Francis congratulates you and walks with you down the long yellow winding path to the point where you started.
21. Sit quietly holding your etheric crystal skull.
22. Then open your eyes and return to the room.

CHAPTER 19

Hall of Learning 1: The Lessons of Balance

For the last 10,000 years humans have been visiting the first Hall of Learning in their efforts to understand and abide by the spiritual laws of Earth. When you receive an invitation from Lady Gaia to incarnate, it automatically includes an offer to visit this particular faculty in the spiritual teaching establishments of this planet.

The colour bathing the students in this temple is a shimmering lilac. Originally the curriculum here included the balance of the seven third-dimensional chakras, and lessons were constantly being represented. However, the energy has now risen. At last, aspirant souls are integrating those lessons and are ready to work with the higher chakras.

Since 2012, specific illumined secrets of the universe have been taught in this Hall of Learning that enable the 12 higher-frequency chakras to work harmoniously together. When individuals are working with these centres, it allows them to live in a golden cocoon of divine perfection.

In addition, in September 2015 Lady Gaia decided to apply instant karma to everyone, whatever their spiritual level, who was currently living on Earth. This has caused many souls to wake up instantly.

The main understanding imparted in this Hall of Learning is about maintaining equilibrium. This is very necessary in a world that allows free will. At the entrance of the hall is the yin–yang symbol of masculine/feminine balance. This symbol opens the gateways of the mind by operating a key within the pineal gland that triggers specific light codes. This enables a person to maintain their equilibrium and find perfect divine masculine and feminine equality within themselves.

Because Earth is still masculine dominated, many highly evolved masters both in and out of incarnation are helping to bring in the divine feminine. They are doing this by whispering higher aspirations into the minds of those who are ready.

Divine masculine energy from Helios is reflected through the Moon. This softens the Sun's stream of light codes with divine feminine love.

In addition, under the direction of Archangel Christiel, the lunar angels are helping to open the petals of the heart.

Christ Light is a feminine energy, and when it is illuminated within the heart centre, it creates balance. Students at this Hall of Learning are taught to bring the keys and codes of the Christ Light from Lakumay, the ascended aspect of Sirius, directly into their heart chakras. This holds their hearts in perfect love. Because the heart affects the mind, this is gradually softening the mindset of those humans who need it.

If two children are sitting on a see-saw and one is heavier than the other, both have to work harder to create stability. As soon as they are absolutely equal in weight, harmonic movement becomes easy and uses less energy.

All the exercises and tests in the first Hall of Learning are about bringing self into balance and then about helping situations, families, countries, the world and ultimately other planets to find stability. This is a practical and at the same time quite challenging ray to deal with. As a result many people are still waiting to move to the second stage, which requires self-love. The training and development offered here require them to practise manipulating energy to create what they want in their lives for the highest good of everyone. The graduate must be able to project mental energy from the higher mind to hold all things in their environment in steadiness. They must also be able to focus divine harmony into distant people, places or situations.

The methods taught and practised here are identical to the mind-training methods developed in Atlantis. The lessons of balance involve letting go of ego, claiming your power and being happy to be equal to others yet different from them. These energies radiate not just from individuals but also in the aura of a planet. At present our planet Earth is trying to balance masculine and feminine energy and those who are attending Lord Kuthumi's training establishments are working to facilitate this.

When perfect balance has been attained, you radiate this in your aura and are ready to undertake the next step. Lady Gaia is waiting with keen anticipation for this colour to develop in the energy fields of Earth so that our planet can transform and help to bring the entire universe into harmony.

Visualization to Visit the Hall of Balance

1. Prepare a space where you can be relaxed and undisturbed. Light a candle if you can.
2. Sit quietly and breathe comfortably with the intention of visiting the Hall of Balance.
3. Focus upon your activated Earth Star.

4. Ask Archangel Michael to place his deep blue cloak of protection around you.
5. Call upon Lord Kuthumi to place a ball round you containing the yin–yang symbol.
6. Visualize yourself rising through time and space to the Hall of Balance in the seventh dimension.
7. The gates bearing a huge yin–yang symbol swing open and you enter a beautiful shimmering golden temple of learning, which is full of students.
8. Lord Kuthumi is standing on a raised platform ready to impart knowledge.
9. Within your left hand you are holding a pure clear crystal skull that links energetically to the vast crystal skull in the centre of the temple.
10. Place the crystal skull on your third eye and sense the symbols within your pineal gland being activated.
11. Be aware of the petals of your heart automatically opening.
12. Sense the energy travelling down to your Earth Star chakra and opening and activating it.
13. Your four-body system is now coming into total balance and equilibrium.
14. Feel the full understanding of balance activating within you as light codes.
15. Relax, and then when you are ready, return to where you started.

In your waking life, as your frequency rises, the information you have received will be readily available to you. Lord Kuthumi will assist with this process whenever you ask him.

You are asked to notice the choices you make to keep your physical life in balance, equilibrium and harmony. Take decisions about how to address this.

All that you learn in your sleep state in the Halls of Learning will be reflected in your daily life, so be aware of changes that are taking place. The reverse is also true. Wise decisions and responses made during the day will immediately impact on and accelerate your progress in the Halls of Learning.

Visualize the yin–yang symbol whenever you feel it is necessary and it will help to realign you.

CHAPTER 20

Hall of Learning 2: The Lessons of Bliss

The path of the ascended master is one of happiness, joy and contentment. It is a state of relaxed harmony that you exude wherever you are. It is your natural state when you are in fifth-dimensional alignment with the Divine.

The most important part of this lesson is to trust the universe to support you. This happens when you absolutely know that your survival needs will be met – in fact more than just met: you know that you will be richly provided for in a loving, nurturing way. So, the foundation teaching provided in this Hall of Learning is the purification and development of the base chakra.

Students only knock for entry on the door of this teaching establishment when their base chakra relaxes and scintillating platinum light pours into it. The keys and codes you receive by entering this temple of education automatically accelerate the ascension of the base chakra into the fourth and fifth dimension.

The entry into this Hall of Learning coincides with the removal of the sixth veil of illusion, which is yellow. This is the second veil to dissolve and this happens when you trust the spirit world to look after you. It is not enough to accept and believe in spiritual help – you must trust it. When you do, the vast spiritual army of invisible helpers that surrounds you will be willing to help you.

Because Earth itself is a mystery school in which our lessons are presented as experiences, the codes of light downloaded into you while you are in the Halls of Learning translate into tests in your daily life. So, while your auric field is absorbing the higher-frequency light, Lord Kuthumi checks that you really are learning the lessons by presenting challenges to you in your physical life. If you can relax and trust that something perfect is being provided for you or that the support you need will come to you, then you have gloriously learned the lesson of this Hall of Learning. When this happens, more and more beautiful platinum light shines out from your base chakra.

These are the steps when you are presented with a challenge:

- Step 1 is to relax and trust that all is in divine right order.
- Step 2 is to listen to the universe. Is this situation bringing you a message from your soul? Are you going in the right direction but your resolve is being tested? Is it time to change your work, your home or something else? Are you being tested about your self-belief or self-worth?
- Step 3 is to take personal mastery and decide clearly which direction your life is to take for the highest good.
- Step 4 is to hold your vision with perfect faith and trust.

The colour that bathes you in this Hall of Learning is a rich, deep platinum infused with diamond lights.

The second phase of lessons here is about the deep contentment that occurs when things are in divine congruence. Earth is a very rare physical planet where we have senses, feelings and emotions. All of these are gifts that were placed here specifically to give us this feeling of happiness:

- Sight is precious. Joyous feelings may arise from watching a soaring bird or seeing our child smile or observing the colours of flowers.
- Hearing is a present from the divine. Listening to the tinkling of a silver stream, hearing the voice of a loved one and absorbing the sound of a choir singing are all designed to bring great contentment.
- Sensation is reserved solely for a physical experience. Everything comes into alignment when we stroke a soft, furry rabbit or float in a warm salty sea or receive a caring massage. Sexual sensation is a special part of this, for orgasm is designed to bring two people together and lift their frequency to a higher dimension. It also holds them for a moment in the now.
- Taste is another sense that is reserved for the Earth experience. To relish a strawberry or mango on a hot day or devour a hot baked potato on a wintry one is a special sensation. With it often comes the other special Earth offering of communal sharing as people eat together.
- To smell a rose or a lily brings us in touch with the angelic forces. To have a whiff of the perfume a passed loved one once wore brings a reminder of them and of the world of spirit. Smells are very evocative and trigger deep memories.

Emotions were originally designed to keep us grounded in our Earth life and to help us take responsibility for ourselves. However, they have become much more than that. They help us move towards or away from situations and people. They allow us to open or close our hearts. They provide the opportunity for the basest or most altruistic responses and huge growth experiences. The choices they offer present opportunities for mastery.

In this Hall of Learning you understand these powerful and extraordinary gifts in a way that engenders immense gratitude. Gratitude is one of the golden keys to universal abundance consciousness, and this lights up your base chakra, making you magnetic to good things.

As soon as your beautiful fifth-dimensional base chakra descends, you are ready to experience bliss. Your fifth-dimensional blueprint is encoded with an acceptance of bliss, which presumes a feeling of safety and inner contentment. This is a frequency that is poured forth from Helios, the Great Central Sun, and the light codes are delivered through the master crystal skull to those who are ready to accept them on a permanent basis.

The symbol for this Hall of Learning is that of the base chakra, the square. This is designed to hold and anchor the bliss of the divine.

The colour bathing the students in this temple is a radiant sunshine yellow. When you absorb this and radiate it from your aura, those who enter your presence feel unaccountably happy.

Visualization to Visit the Hall of Bliss

1. Prepare a space where you can be relaxed and undisturbed. Light a candle if you can.
2. Sit quietly and breathe comfortably with the intention of visiting the Hall of Bliss.
3. Focus upon your activated Earth Star.
4. Ask Archangel Michael to place his deep blue cloak of protection around you.

5. Find yourself standing in a perfect square that is radiating sunshine yellow.
6. You are in the courtyard of the second Hall of Learning and Lord Kuthumi himself is waiting for you, smiling a warm welcome.
7. Although you are surrounded by fellow students, you feel alone with Lord Kuthumi, who places his hand on your heart so that your 12 chakras spin faster in readiness for a download of divine bliss.
8. Become aware of the vast citrine and platinum crystal skull on a raised dais in the centre of the temple.
9. Hold your personal crystal skull in front of you and use all your senses to see, hear, smell and taste the stream of light containing sacred geometric symbols and light codes pouring from the central skull into your skull and then into all your chakras.
10. This is activating your crown and base chakra in alignment with the bliss of true ascended mastery.
11. You may feel a burst of happiness, joy, safety and trust in the universe or these feelings may seep gradually into you.
12. Return slowly to where you started, giving yourself time to absorb the higher light codes and feelings associated with them.
13. Trust the universe is supporting you totally and look for the joy in everything.

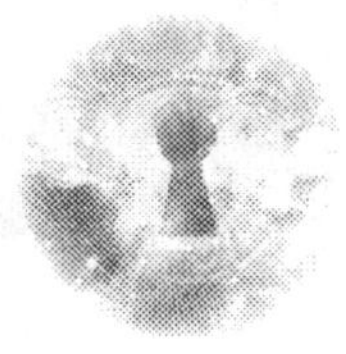

CHAPTER 21

Hall of Learning 3: Understanding Crystal Technology

In the time of Golden Atlantis, everyone had 12 radiant spinning chakras with 12 strands of active DNA and as a result of holding fifth-dimensional energies, their bodies were silicon-based. Silicon-based bodies hold more high-frequency light than third-dimensional carbon-based ones. Light carries spiritual information and knowledge, so the more light you hold, the more keys and codes to spiritual understanding are available to you.

Because of this, the High Priests and Priestesses were able to receive extraordinary material from the Intergalactic Council. This included information about the properties of crystals and how to co-operate with the elemental beings within them. They then passed the appropriate information to the people. This was the great secret of the power of Golden Atlantis.

It was also helpful that the people then used 90 per cent of their much larger brain capacity. Currently we use 10 per cent of our much smaller brains.

In this Hall of Learning, students learn about the transformation of a third-dimensional carbon-based world into a high-frequency silicon-based one. They understand the energetic properties of carbon, which holds only a small amount of relatively low-frequency light, and its expansion into crystalline form. This transformation is an automatic consequence of raising your frequency to a certain level. In addition they learn about the use of sacred geometry within the crystalline form to make extraordinary things happen that are currently beyond our comprehension. Many people are currently visiting this particular Hall of Learning to bring back an understanding of crystal technology for the new Golden Age.

The colour bathing the students in this temple is shimmering golden peach. This colour is a synthesis of golden wisdom and pink love with a diamond sparkle.

The people of Atlantis could tune into many different frequency bands. For example, they could easily switch their internal dials to the wavelengths of angels, unicorns, elementals, trees and animals. When they did this, they could communicate directly with these beings with their thoughts, pictures or senses. This was accomplished with intention, helped by the fact that the Atlanteans were clairvoyant, clairaudient and telepathic, so that they were already tuned into other species.

Nowadays people are regaining these psychic abilities without even realizing it. You may not hear a voice, but you receive an impression. You may not see a vivid picture, but you have a sense of what is happening. You may have a pretty good idea of what people are thinking. This means you are psychic and you may well experience claircognizance, which is high-frequency knowing. For enlightened mastery, your task is to accept and trust.

Within every crystal is an elemental, a tiny spirit from the nature world, who is open to connecting with you. When you get to know and love a crystal, you can learn to communicate with the elemental being, who will respond to your loving commands and wishes. For example, the elemental may work with the crystal to light it up when you ask it to. This is how they lit their homes in the Golden Era of Atlantis.

Everything that our computers can do nowadays was done in that time by programming crystals directly with the power of the mind through the elemental in the crystal.

Some crystals become the energetic homes of highly evolved beings who transmit important information, healing or other qualities through the medium of the crystal. As Golden Atlantis progressed, the people were able to tune into the very potent essences residing in powerful crystals. As soon as the inhabitants were ready, the Intergalactic Council downloaded the blueprints for almost unbelievable high-vibration technology into the great temple crystals. This was absorbed and worked on by the Magi, who then explained it to the people. In this way rockets were built that moved at speeds faster than we can conceive. A multi-level system of flying transportation was developed. Advanced hydroponics were set up to grow crops with very little effort from people. The Atlanteans controlled the weather; they used laser surgery; they regrew limbs; they built circular buildings and communicated with other star systems. They even accessed minerals from other star systems to use in this one. They did this by dematerializing it, drawing it to Earth and rematerializing it. All was powered by energy drawn from the Great Crystal housed within the Temple of Poseidon, which was in turn powered by pure Source energy.

At the same time the people lived lives of extreme simplicity, harmony, fun, relaxation, creativity and loving interaction, mostly out in nature. Their minds were clear and calm so that they could focus and manifest in a way that is currently beyond our capability. But the basis of their technology was communicating with the life-forces within crystals, using the power of mind control, sound, light and visualization.

When you enter the temple of crystal technology, these gifts, talents and powers, which are encoded in your fifth-dimensional blueprint from Atlantis, will start to wake up. You are asked to remain alert to seed thoughts being dropped into your mind. Lord Kuthumi will help you, and so will Lord Hilarion, who is overseeing the return of the crystal technology of Atlantis.

Remember to thank crystals, including the intelligent spirits within your own computer crystals. Like all sentient beings, they respond to human emotions.

Visualization to Visit the Hall of Crystal Technology

1. Prepare a space where you can be relaxed and undisturbed.
2. Light a candle and dedicate it to the return of crystal technology on Earth for the highest good of all.
3. Focus upon your activated Earth Star.
4. Ask Archangel Michael to place his deep blue cloak of protection around you.
5. A small circular flying machine is landing beside you. You enter it and are transported silently and instantly to the Hall of Crystal Technology.
6. You exit the transport and find yourself in the courtyard of the hall. You can see many other beings arriving in the same way.
7. You can see a glorious golden peach colour shimmering through an arch, so you follow the other students through the archway and into the hall. You are immediately bathed in glittering golden peach.
8. Lord Kuthumi and Lord Hilarion stand side by side on a dais and greet everyone by raising their hands. From their palms a bright golden peach ray hits you in the third eye.

9. As you sit and absorb this light, you find yourself holding a crystal. Feel it, sense it and hold it to your third eye. Become aware of the elemental being within the crystal.
10. Lovingly ask the elemental being to light up the crystal. Immediately your crystal and every other one in the hall ignites, creating a fairyland of lights.
11. Lord Kuthumi and Lord Hilarion are now sending you a picture of some future spiritual technology. Relax and let something drop into your mind.
12. By receiving this as a sacred trust, you are helping to change the collective consciousness so that it can manifest more quickly and easily for the highest good of humanity and the planet.
13. Thank Lord Kuthumi and Lord Hilarion and return to the central courtyard where your flying transport is waiting to take you back to where you started.

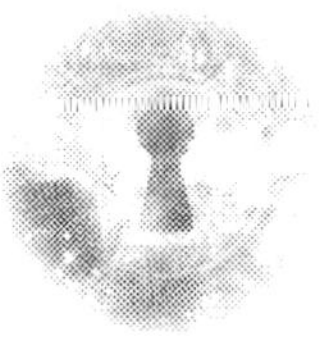

CHAPTER 22

Hall of Learning 4: The Vibration of Truth

Lord Kuthumi has always been interested in the great immutable spiritual laws that govern Earth. These describe how everything from karma to grace to responsibility responds to vibration.

The vibration of pure truth is shimmering, sparkling radiant white. It emanates from a wholesome heart and mind as well as total alignment with the Divine. When you carry this shimmering white vibration in your aura, everyone feels its resonance and trusts you. It gives people around you a feeling of safety and hope. On a day-by-day basis, every time you speak and act with total honesty and integrity, more white light builds in your energy fields.

Students who study in this temple are bathed in perfect white light that fizzes and sparkles in every cell of the body and is forever carried in the aura.

In this temple you learn about the different inner child strategies that humans develop to survive and to protect themselves. An understanding of this engenders huge compassion in the hearts of all. This in turn opens the pure white petals of the higher heart as you see humanity and the vulnerable aspect of yourself with new eyes.

The child who learns to please their parents in order to receive love and attention, for example, has to suppress their own wants. They subtly tell untruths in order to stay popular but feel angry because they cannot be their own authentic self. They become a pleasing, compliant adult, but people don't really trust them because they will offer the answer they think people want to hear rather than the honest one. A download of light into the throat and solar plexus chakras through the temple skull will enable a student like this to receive the courage to speak their truth. For those whose entire survival strategy is based on a silken web of lies, the teachings of this Hall of Learning may be extremely difficult to digest, but when they do so, their growth will inevitably be great.

The child who feels they must be first or at the top of the class in order to receive parental approval, on the other hand, drives and strives. Unless they heal their inner child, when they are an adult they will burn out in their quest to do anything possible to win. Success sometimes becomes such an all-consuming struggle that integrity is lost on the way. As an adult, this person's emotional survival depends on doing well, even if their parents are dead. For them, a download of light into the heart enables them to feel loved. This means they can do their best while enjoying life and maintaining their inner integrity.

The child who learns to manipulate with food or lies or in any other way to get attention also loses integrity, and eventually this earns karma. The person who is still driven by this inner child doesn't really know who they are and needs a full chakra bath in order to clear the survival mechanisms they have adopted. Then they can be themselves.

If a child has to be perfect for their parents, they will do anything to hide all those aspects of themselves that they perceive as imperfect. These become their shadow when they are an adult. Very often the adult with such an inner child will not try, for fear of failing. Again, a full chakra bath will wash out the fear of not being good enough.

Every single adult human being has an inner child who is needy. Unhappy people have created a critical, judgemental or punitive inner parental voice, so they constantly dismiss or undermine their own inner beauty. This has often been passed on through generations.

The higher spiritual realms have great compassion and sympathy for all of us and are now helping us to find our inner truth and beauty. This period to the new Golden Age in 2032 marks the end of the hurting inner child. It is time to change and create happy inner personalities.

The great masters who have lived in a physical body still have an inner child. It is part of the Earth experience. However, they have developed a wise inner self who encourages, loves and helps the vulnerable part of themselves.

And when you access the Hall of Truth, the keys and codes of the authentic self pour into you and wash away the old compulsions that were based on lack of love. Then you can live in truth with a wise, honest inner self.

Pure White Truth

There are certain beings and groups who have developed pure white truth and can impart the sacred understandings of it to others.

Unicorns are known as the purest of the pure because they vibrate with divine truth. They are able to take the desires and visions of your soul to Source for higher activation. They teach vibrationally in this temple and when you surrender yourself and receive their input, it can be a transformational experience.

The Great White Brotherhood, which includes all White Brotherhoods, was set up by Lord Kuthumi and is now under the direction of Lord Maitreya. It consists of those beings who have earned the pure white colour of truth, integrity, honour, peace and high intention. They radiate diamond white in their auras. Lord Maitreya and other members of this illustrious band teach in this temple.

Archangel Gabriel carries the diamond of truth in his energy fields and is personally able to place this over you when you graduate from this Hall of Learning.

And Serapis Bey carries the pure White Flame of Atlantis, which he can place over the energy fields of those who are ready.

Visualization to Visit the Hall of Truth

1. Prepare a space where you can be relaxed and undisturbed. Light a candle if you can.
2. Sit quietly and breathe comfortably with the intention of visiting the Hall of Truth.
3. Focus upon your activated Earth Star.
4. Ask Archangel Michael to place his deep blue cloak of protection around you.
5. Find yourself standing at the vast glittering white gates of the temple of truth.
6. As you step into the great hall, you find yourself within a shimmering, shining, multifaceted white diamond. It is lighting up your true essence.
7. Serapis Bey steps forwards and places the White Ascension Flame of Atlantis over you. Stand in it as it clears and lights up your 12 chakras.
8. A mighty, majestic, pure white unicorn alights beside you and pours

magical shimmering white light over you.

9. Finally, Lord Kuthumi places one hand on your heart and the other on your third eye so that you feel the old illusions burning up in an alchemical burst of white fire and your heart lighting up with the joy of truth.
10. You have received the gift of being yourself. You can be true to yourself.
11. You radiate the white light of pure truth.
12. When you are ready, thank Lord Kuthumi and return to where you started.

From now on relax and speak your truth and you will be trusted and honoured wherever you go.

Here is a visualization to create wise, positive, loving, supporting, encouraging, helpful inner parents. They may look like your own parents or they may appear completely different. When you have met them, start to integrate them into your life on a daily basis until they become part of your new reality.

Visualization to Create Wise, Positive, Loving Inner Parents for Yourself

1. Sit quietly where you can be relaxed and undisturbed.
2. Visualize the golden Christ Light pouring into your heart.
3. Be aware of a huge white house in the sky above you.
4. White steps lead down from the house to where you are sitting and a strong blue light is approaching down the steps.
5. Out of the light steps a strong, wise, smiling, protective father.
6. You tell him your problems and he encourages, supports and helps you. He reminds you that you are special and clever and he loves you exactly as you are.

7. He sits beside you and you can feel his support and strength. Relax.
8. And now a pink light is approaching down the steps.
9. Out of the pink light steps a warm, wise, happy, loving mother.
10. She puts her arms round you and tells you that you are perfect and loved and beautiful or handsome.
11. She encourages you and reminds you she loves you exactly as you are. Nothing can stop her from loving you.
12. You sit between your strong, wise, loving father and warm, wise, loving mother and feel safe and supported.
13. Think of your home and work life and listen to their positive input and loving support.
14. From now on, whenever you are afraid or lonely or feel you aren't good enough, listen to their voices.

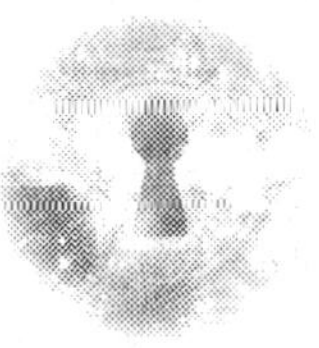

CHAPTER 23

Hall of Learning 5: Codes Hidden within Nature

Being surrounded by the natural world is one of the delights and blessings of life on Earth. The responsibility of humanity is to take care of the trees and plants, as well as the animals, birds and insects they support.

The mighty ninth-dimensional Master Pan looks after the natural world, overseeing the elementals and helping nature to flourish on Earth. A few years ago Diana met him while out walking in the forest. He stood still in a great shining light and looked quietly at her. She was mesmerized and could not move while he downloaded keys and codes into her. And then he disappeared, leaving her to walk quietly on in a state of wonder and amazement.

Archangel Purlimiek has come from another universe to help nature ascend. He radiates a beautiful green-blue light and watches over the green world. If a tree is being chopped down unnecessarily, his angels will whisper to the woodcutter in an effort to prevent its fall.

These two mighty beings, Master Pan and Archangel Purlimiek, often work with Lord Kuthumi in his Halls of

Learning to help souls throughout the universes to understand the secret codes hidden within nature.

Our planet was constructed as a mystery school where answers could be found in many places, particularly within nature. Green was the colour of choice for nature because it synthesized the blue of Source love through the Pleiades with the soft, pale yellow of the intellect and the happy sunshine yellow of the Sun. It isn't by chance that in the spring, the time of birth and renewal, the new leaves are a hope-filled, sunny, yellow green.

Green is the colour of balance, and this vibration holds and supports all life on this planet. Where people live surrounded by trees and grass, they feel happier and calmer.

The Fibonacci sequence and the golden section are the sacred geometry governing the growth of a tree, a flower, a snail and much of nature. Sacred geometry attracts angel sonics. This means that angels sing over anything constructed according to these special divine proportions and purify the energy round it. For example, when this geometry is used to erect a cathedral, the angel harmonics within the sacred building allow miracles to happen. Miracles also happen under trees and around plants, but we are less aware of them.

Plants are carefully encoded. Healing plants, for example, are coded with the geometry of divinely perfect human organs. As an illustration, when a person with a defective liver ingests the herb for the perfect liver, the healthy fifth-dimensional blueprint within the herb overlays the liver and realigns it to total health. Other plants and herbs have been provided by the Intergalactic Council to bring about perfect memory or deep relaxation. In the Golden Era of Atlantis, when people had no karma, ingesting plants was enough to bring them into perfect balance and radiant health again very quickly.

The perfume of flowers and plants was designed to affect receptors within the human brain and open us up to love, peace, relaxation, joy and divine contentment. Certain flowers, like the lily and the rose, help us to connect with the resonance of angels.

The natural world is looked after by the elemental kingdom. The little creatures who work with the air, earth, water and fire enable the bird, animal and human kingdoms to survive and flourish. Many of these elementals only contain one element, but there are others who have more than one element in their make-up. Elementals are evolving, as are we.

- Air elementals include sylphs, who work with the wind and keep the roots of plants free, and little esaks, who have arrived recently from another universe to help clear pollution on our planet. Fairies, too, are air elementals. They assist the flowers to grow and also support the work of the angels, archangels and unicorns. Since the Cosmic Moment in 2012, many of the light, fun-filled and beautiful fairies have ascended to become angels.

- Earth elementals who work with the soil are pixies and gnomes, while those who help the trees are elves. Very wise goblins, who are also earth elementals, have highly evolved heart centres.

- Water elementals include mermaids, who look after the water plants, undines, who keep rivers and oceans clear, and kyhils, who have arrived recently from another universe to help consume the pollution in the waters of the planet.

- Salamanders are fire elementals who keep flames alive.

- And imps and fauns help with the process of photosynthesis. They are a combination of earth, air and water.

- Dragons, too, are made up of a combination of elements. They have been human companions and helpers for aeons and are returning now to help us and the planet in our ascension process.

So many experiences are offered on the physical plane of Earth, including the delights of nature, that an incarnation is regarded with awe throughout the universes. And many beings wish to visit this particular Hall of Learning.

The teaching course provided here is vast and eclectic. Certain birds sing notes to attune people to their fifth-dimensional blueprint. Ants teach about building codes. Spiders demonstrate overcoming gravity with intention.

The symbol that allows you entry to the secrets of nature is a green spiral, while the colours bathing the students in this Hall of Learning are pale translucent marigold and hundreds of shades of green. When these colours are in your aura, you work with nature and the elementals and they automatically respond to you.

Visualization to Visit the Hall of Nature

1. Prepare a space where you can be relaxed and undisturbed. Light a candle if you can.
2. Sit quietly and breathe comfortably with the intention of visiting the Hall of Nature.
3. Focus upon your activated Earth Star.
4. Ask Archangel Michael to place his deep blue cloak of protection around you.
5. Visualize that you are walking slowly through a green spiral until you find yourself standing in the centre of a beautiful green glade. Colourful wild

flowers grow among the grass, a stream tinkles and shimmers, birds sing and animals rustle as they play.

6. The mighty Master Pan steps forwards, smiling. He touches your third eye with his hand.
7. Consciously or unconsciously, you become aware of the sacred geometry in the trunks of the trees, in the petals of the flowers, in the shells of the snails and in everything around you. As you do so, you hear angels singing, and this lights up everything.
8. You become aware of a green-blue light as the magnificent Archangel Purlimiek, the angel of nature, hovers over the glade, pouring his essence over this magical place.
9. Immediately you are aware of pixies and elves sitting on the branches of the trees. A wise goblin waves to you, while imps and fairies and sylphs whirl round you. Hundreds of elementals, like sparks of light, twirl and dance in the glade. Golden dragons circle round the glade, protecting the energy.
10. Lord Kuthumi, the World Teacher himself, appears in the middle of the flower-strewn grass. He raises his hands and a most beautiful perfume fills the air. The scent of roses, lilies, lilies of the valley, scented stocks and a dozen other high-frequency perfumes float on the air, inducing happiness and love.
11. Breathe the perfume in. Whether you are aware of it or not, it is affecting your brainwaves and opening you even more to the secrets of nature.
12. Thank Master Pan, Archangel Purlimiek and Lord Kuthumi, then find yourself exiting through the spiral back to where you started.
13. Be prepared to see all of nature with shining new eyes and a glowing heart.

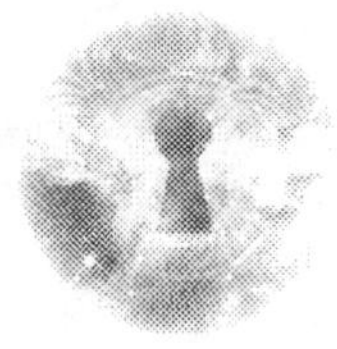

CHAPTER 24

Hall of Learning 6: Unconditional Love

In the sixth Hall of Learning Lord Kuthumi oversees teachings about all the different facets of love and how to bring them all into pure, Christed, transcendent love.

He has invited the great Universal Angel Mary, who brings Source love directly through the Cosmic Heart, to overlight the teachings here, and many great masters and goddesses, including Mother Mary, St Clare, St Catherine of Siena, Quan Yin, St Teresa d'Ávila, Jesus and St Germain, co-operate with her. They all carry in their energy fields the Christ Light, the golden-white ninth-dimensional vibration of pure unconditional love.

Each type of love, whether it is a mother's love or the love between a husband and wife or partners, the love a child has for their parents, the love between friends or any other kind of heart connection, is signified by different sacred geometry within the heart chakra. But all are illuminated by golden-white light and the pale aquamarine of the Universal Angel Mary.

When a heart feels hurt for whatever reason, the sacred geometry of divine love within the pure white centre of the heart is distorted, depending on the nature of the original perceived wound. Hurts are based on two egos in conflict in order to learn. At a soul level, the two have contracted for this to occur. No one can do anything to you without your soul agreement, and there are always many lessons involved. And the other person's Higher Self will be watching with love and compassion and total amity. The same applies even if the two people are strangers on Earth. We are all one at a soul level.

Within the Hall of Unconditional Love work is taking place to heal 10,000 years of old ways of perceiving love and emotions. It is time now for transformation.

At this moment, for the first time since the Golden Era of Atlantis, there is a move in the spiritual realms to flood Earth with the unconditional love of the Christ Light. This entails a process of deconstruction of old beliefs. Then comes the reconstruction of the template of pure and open heart centres. It is awesome!

Many great Illumined Masters, including those we have mentioned – Mother Mary, St Clare, St Catherine of Siena, Quan Yin, St Teresa d'Ávila, Jesus and St Germain – are lighting up hearts and minds on the inner planes to help us comprehend that a true spiritual path embraces and accepts all religions, that everything is perfect so there is nothing to forgive and that love is the natural human state.

Universal Angel Mary and her co-teachers are educating those who attend this Hall of Unconditional Love about different healing methods, all of which open heart centres and bring them into alignment with the Cosmic Heart.

The heart has 33 chambers or petals, the number of the Cosmic Heart and the Christ consciousness. The outer 10 of these are green when we are moving through our lessons and our hearts are yet to open. Then, with the stirrings of love for animals, others and self, the petals become pink. As qualities such as compassion, caring and forgiveness grow and develop, the next layer of spiritual pink–violet petals unfurl. And then there are the petals of unconditional and transcendent love, connection with the Cosmic Heart, cosmic love and finally oneness, as the petals become pure white. Then our heart centre becomes a fragrant open white rose and we radiate pure love wherever we are. We are a walking master.

The colour bathing the students in this Hall of Learning is the divine feminine energy of shimmering, pale, aquamarine white shot through with translucent pale pink and deep gold. When this frequency is encapsulated in our aura and becomes part of who we are, it radiates from our energy fields. Then we automatically spread a higher spiritual understanding. We become a holder of cosmic love.

Visualization to Visit the Hall of Unconditional Love

1. Prepare a space where you can be relaxed and undisturbed. Light a candle if you can.
2. Sit quietly and breathe comfortably with the intention of visiting the Hall of Unconditional Love.
3. Focus upon your activated Earth Star.
4. Ask Archangel Michael to place his deep blue cloak of protection around you.
5. You are standing in a green meadow at the start of a path that shimmers as it spirals up and round a hill.
6. As you walk you are watching the green fields that line the path. Suddenly the Sun rises and the meadows are lit with gold. Everything is stunningly beautiful and something shifts in your heart.
7. You become aware that pink flowers carpet the path and meadows. As the Sun shimmers onto them, it lights up many humans and animals that you normally do not notice. Instantly your heart lights up with great love

for all your fellow creatures.

8. And as you walk on, the flowers shine with a hint of violet as the Sun pours through the violet angels who are now surrounding you. Your heart is opening with compassion and empathy for those who are on Earth. You really care what happens to them.
9. You are nearing the summit of the hill and can see the end of your spiral path glowing in pure white light.
10. The magnificent Universal Angel Mary is singing over you, along with the great masters Mother Mary, St Clare, St Catherine of Siena, Quan Yin, St Teresa d'Ávila, Jesus and St Germain, filling your heart with codes of pure love. Open your arms and breathe it all in.
11. Your heart is a pure, white, fifth-dimensional rose that is fully open. You may smell its perfume.
12. From the summit of your hill you look down and see that the ego selves of people are in conflict. With enlightened eyes, you observe that their Higher Selves are holding hands.
13. You radiate love to everyone. There is only love. You are one with everyone.
14. A gossamer cloak of pale aquamarine white shot through with translucent pale pink and deep gold falls over your energy fields.
15. At last it is time to return to where you started, with your shimmering, glowing diamond heart wide open and radiant.

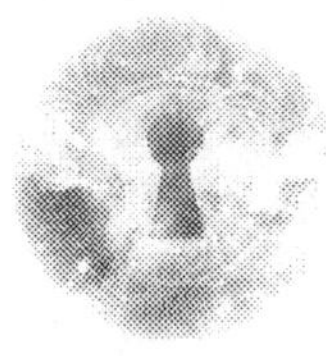

CHAPTER 25

Hall of Learning 7: Higher Perception

The beings who attend this faculty of learning are ready for advanced enlightenment. They know that everything on Earth is perfect, for life here is a great experiment where the rules are precise. However, it is one thing to know this intellectually; it is another to feel it in our essence and be able to apply it in our own life. Everything follows spiritual law. So how can we change our perspective about some of the things happening on Earth? In this hall, the students see everything from an enlightened viewpoint.

Remember that nothing can happen to anyone unless their soul permits it. If someone is experiencing density or challenges, it is arising for one of several reasons.

A major one is that souls are wishing to pay off karma, especially at this time, as the current 20-year period offers opportunities for spiritual growth never before seen in any of the universes.

On this planet the basic law of karma – as you give, so shall you receive – still rules supreme, and this applies over lifetimes. We are now living in end times. From now until 2032 there is a final opportunity to complete karma on this plane of existence before the new Golden Age commences. At a soul level, literally billions of beings desire to settle their debts and set themselves free. They really want to learn their lessons so that they can take advantage of the cosmic promotions now on offer. Those who are ready and spiritually balanced will have the amazing opportunity to participate in the new Golden Age on Earth.

Here are some higher perspectives on other challenging life experiences.

A soul may be valiant and giving, so undertaking huge trials in order to give others experiences that will enable them to ascend to the next golden phase of Earth. For example, a person may agree at a soul level to be disabled so that their loved ones can learn about selfless giving and caring and build many high-frequency qualities in their auras. The disabled one's soul may want to learn patience or about relinquishing control or dependence and gratitude. These may not be decisions based on karma, but a desire for growth, or even an initiation into a much higher frequency. Many of the harsh challenges that old souls are choosing to undertake are crucifixions and initiations.

Nothing can be done to you unless all the participating souls in the drama have agreed. You cannot die in a particular way unless your Higher Self has contracted to partake in that story.

Very often the participants in dire situations and relationships are soul mates who have undertaken to teach each other important lessons. Many years ago Diana had a very difficult relationship with her mother, now long passed. She tried every way to resolve it, but it seemed impossible. Then one night as she lay in bed she saw the Higher Self of her mother enter the room. The woman was radiant with light and looked at her with great love and caring. Instantly Diana knew this was her mum's true self and the stuff they had built between them on Earth was an illusion, and it changed her perception of her completely. After that, whenever the ego stuff reared its head, she was able to remember that the battle was between her mother's hurt self and her own hurt self. She would think about the love pouring from her mother's Higher Self and smile and let go.

The first understanding of this Hall of Learning is that there is no blame, no guilt and nothing ever to forgive or grieve for.

This is the seventh Hall of Learning and the number seven is the angelic vibration, so here students learn to see through angelic eyes, that is, from a seventh-dimensional perspective. When an angel looks at you, they see only the higher frequencies you radiate, your highest potential and the desires of your soul. As they hold the blueprint of this great intention and hope, they help you achieve it.

Students in this hall also learn that when you place the divine blueprint of love over a person or situation, this starts to heal your distorted visions and understanding. When enough people do this, it transforms beliefs and mends the broken keys and codes of love and realigns them in order to restore the divine plan.

Holding a pure intention for someone else also assists that person in accomplishing their goals. You can help someone to achieve their vision by keeping it with them or for them.

Diana once had a letter from someone who had read her books. This man had a son whom he described as lazy and uninterested in scholarly achievement. However, the boy was bright. The father had tried everything to motivate him into achieving his potential, but to no avail. He asked if Diana would hold the vision of the boy doing well at school. She agreed and put out a clear picture to the universe of the boy relaxed, happy and doing really well at school. She said she really shouldn't have been surprised at the result, but she was. At the end of term the boy was top in his class in all subjects and had been chosen to play for the school football team. Furthermore, he was motivated and happy.

The father's desire for his son was coloured with exasperation and his own hopes and attachments. Because she had never met the child, Diana held the vision without attachment and for the highest good of another, so spiritual law automatically kicked in. This is why it is often a help to ask someone who is not connected to you to hold a picture of what you want to achieve or attract.

Pure diamond white laced with gold and pale transcendent pink bathes the students in this faculty, and when you hold these colours and their associated light in your aura, people trust your wisdom and listen to you. Furthermore, you help them achieve their divine potential.

Visualization to Visit the Hall of Higher Perception

1. Prepare a space where you can be relaxed and undisturbed. Light a candle if you can.
2. Sit quietly and breathe comfortably with the intention of visiting the Hall of Higher Perception.
3. Focus upon your activated Earth Star.
4. Ask Archangel Michael to place his deep blue cloak of protection around you.
5. Focus on your heart and see it shimmering with pure white, laced with hints of pure gold and pale pink.
6. You are standing outside the temple gates, which bear a large illuminated diamond symbol. Light from your heart beams into the diamond shape and unlocks the gates, which swing open.
7. As you enter, Lord Kuthumi and hundreds of beautiful angels greet you with smiles and open hearts.

8. The crystal skull in the centre of the hall beams extraordinary energy to you that you have never experienced before. It hits you in your third eye.
9. The centre of the hall swings open, revealing a hole through which you can see down to the Earth.
10. Angels sing over you, keeping your frequency high as you see aspects of your life from a divine perspective.
11. More angels gather over you, singing, as you look down at some difficult situations on Earth. See them with angelic eyes.
12. Beam the blueprint of divine perfection from your third eye into a difficult situation and see all the participants acting with peace and love, as they truly are in the ascended realms.
13. Thank Lord Kuthumi and the angels and return to where you started.

CHAPTER 26

Hall of Learning 8: Universal Oneness

Lord Kuthumi has invited one of the greatest Illumined Universal Masters to teach in this Hall of Learning: Lord Kumeka. He has recently ascended into the 11th dimension. He has served in many universes and was part of the team that set up and oversaw the fifth and final experiment of Atlantis, during which the Golden Age arose.

In response to the great clarion call to help Earth during this unprecedented 20-year transformation, Lord Kumeka has returned here in charge of the Eighth Ray, the ray of deep cleansing, transformation, joy and oneness. Through this wonderful, luminous topaz blue ray, he is helping individuals on Earth go through deep purification so that they are ready to link into universal Oneness. This brings about a feeling of transcendent joy and peace. He works with us when we are living mainly in the fifth dimension.

Visualization to Receive Lord Kumeka's Topaz Ray of Transformation

1. Prepare a space where you can be relaxed and undisturbed. Light a candle if you can.
2. Sit quietly and breathe comfortably with the intention of visiting the Hall of Higher Perception.
3. Focus upon your activated Earth Star.
4. Ask Archangel Michael to place his deep blue cloak of protection around you. As you approach this hall, you will be aware of bright light pouring from it. You will see the infinity symbol, like a sideways figure of eight, on the vast blue and gold gates, which open automatically when you walk towards them with pure intention in your heart.
5. When you have passed through the gates, you find yourself standing in an enormous ball of translucent topaz blue light. Within it are the perfect codes for you as an upper fifth-dimensional being.
6. You are holding your personal crystal or crystal skull, and as you wait quietly in this rarefied Hall of Learning, you receive a download of esoteric information through it. This will not come to you consciously. Just relax and allow it to filter into your energy fields.
7. As this happens, your essence is overlaid with the blueprint of your ascended master perfection for this lifetime. This is an awesome opportunity to open your heart and surrender yourself to the utmost possibilities for your incarnation. Entering this hall requires you to surrender any limiting self-beliefs held in your personal ego, for it starts to loosen them by bringing memories and the associated emotions to the surface. Then the gold light brings forwards your higher wisdom.
8. Your monad or I AM Presence is your 12th-dimensional aspect. We all have the blueprint of this unbelievably illuminated higher part of us hidden in the codes of our hearts. When you are ready, the link to your

monadic wisdom will start to activate. Stand in this Hall of Universal Oneness and ask Lord Kuthumi and Lord Kumeka to harmonize the vibrations.

At the 12th-dimensional monadic level we are all one. There is only the light and love of Source, the song of the Seraphim and joy beyond our current understanding. It may be out of our reach now, but have you ever looked at a sky covered in cloud so dense and thick that it is hard to imagine anything else? Then suddenly, just for a moment, the cloud parts and you catch a tantalizing glimpse of sparkling blue sky. It reveals promise and hope. It reminds you of half-forgotten possibilities.

A visit to the Hall of Universal Oneness under the tutelage of Lord Kumeka ignites this energy of promise and hope within you. It is available to you now.

One day Diana was walking quietly in the forest when she mentally asked Lord Kumeka and Lord Kuthumi for permission to enter the Hall of Universal Oneness. This was granted. She then had a very interesting, uncomfortable but profound experience. As the vast blue and gold gates swung open, she immediately found herself in a topaz crystal ball. For some time she walked along the leafy paths in the physical world surrounded by this extraordinary transparent blue ball of energy and found old memories surfacing. Feelings that she hadn't experienced for years but had been clearly locked in her cells at an inner child and teenage age rose from the depth of her being. Old sad, powerless feelings that she had forgotten were being cleansed and transmuted as she walked.

When this was done, Lord Kumeka asked her repeatedly what she really wanted and she told him of all the things that brought her joy. At last, gold light shimmered and sparkled around her and she felt something deep had been shifted. That was when the blueprint for her ascended master perfection was laid over her auric field and she was touched with a magical, elusive promise of possibilities.

When you want to build a house, you start with a picture in your mind. Then you discuss it with the architect and the drawings are completed and agreed on. At last you can truly envision the outcome. Then you have to do the work to activate it. Your next task is to build and inhabit that house! As long as you have done this for the highest good of all, it will be a place of joy and happiness.

Visualization to Visit the Hall of Universal Oneness

1. Prepare a space where you can be relaxed and undisturbed. Light a candle if you can.
2. Sit quietly and breathe comfortably into your heart centre, feeling yourself surrender to the higher energy.
3. Focus upon your activated Earth Star.
4. Ask Archangel Michael to place his deep blue cloak of protection around you.
5. Be aware you are rising through the dimensions, through a beautiful shimmering colour spectrum beyond anything you have ever seen.
6. Ahead of you are great blue and gold gates with a figure of eight symbol on them.
7. Mentally run your finger over the figure of eight as you ask Lord Kuthumi and Lord Kumeka for permission to visit the Hall of Universal Oneness.
8. The gates swing open. Lord Kuthumi stands on one side of the hall radiating yellow gold light. Lord Kumeka stands on the other side of the hall radiating blue light.

9. In the centre is an enormous luminous transparent topaz ball. Step into it.
10. Surrender to the deep cleansing that is taking place. You may sense or feel the old stuff surfacing to be transmuted.
11. Lord Kuthumi raises a hand and you receive a download of codes that are perfect for the next phase of your evolution.
12. Lord Kumeka raises a hand and you sense a gossamer cloak containing the blueprint of your ascended master perfection falling over your aura.
13. Look up and see a tiny pinprick of immensely high-frequency pure light. It is igniting hope and joy within you.
14. The two great Lords of Light touch your heart, which becomes hundreds of times brighter than it was before.
15. Thank the Lords of Light. Thank Source for the grace of this moment.
16. Return to where you started and relax so that you absorb the experience.

CHAPTER 27

Hall of Learning 9: Service with Joy

When your fifth-dimensional heart opens, it becomes a joy and delight to serve others, your community and the world for the highest good. In fact it confers such bliss on you that you radiate light that can be visible to others.

Because of this, service with joy is one of the greatest ascension paths. It attracts many aspirants. If you decide this is your spiritual journey, you will enjoy soaking in the teachings of this Hall of Learning.

Service with joy does not need to be the single focus of your golden ascension path. You may wish it to be part of your essence whatever path you choose. Either way, you can enter Lord Kuthumi's school of learning to attend this course before you decide whether or not this is right for you.

Lord Kuthumi has invited Archangel Metatron to teach with him in this hall. Archangel Metatron's light, wisdom and knowledge are encoded into the central teaching crystal skull, so that this extraordinary luminous skull radiates alternately Archangel Metatron's golden orange light and Lord Kuthumi's profound yellow light.

Before you can appreciate the wonder of this training course, you must feel and understand oneness. It is only when your heart is open to the hearts of every sentient being that you truly experience the deepest connection with Source and all beings everywhere. This is when you connect with Source love. This is the true ascension gift that Archangel Metatron and Lord Kuthumi are bringing to those who sincerely aspire to serve with joy as an ascended master.

Because the most beautiful golden orange and yellow light bathes the students who graduate from this course, they glow with contentment and happiness. When you carry this colour in your aura, you automatically spread higher ascension teachings and love to others.

Many people in the caring professions are students or graduates of this Hall of Learning. Their souls have placed them in their position. Those who fulfil their tasks with serenity and joy are completing in their day work what their spirits are learning during their sleep time.

Many old people are agreeing to live longer now in order to give their children or carers the opportunity to open their hearts as they look after them so that they can graduate from this Hall of Learning. At a soul level all is perfect.

Many animals have ascended quickly in comparison with humans. One of the reasons is that they serve with uncomplicated joy. If you are cross with your dog, the next time it sees you, it wags its tail in joy, absolutely delighted to be with you again. Animals' hearts are wide open and they do not process with the left brain. They live in the present, with the wisdom and divine feminine acceptance of the right brain.

Service with joy entails living in the heart, in the now, with total acceptance and simple wisdom. With every out-breath, you offer blessings and grace.

Within the teaching temple, the sacred geometric codes that flow into you from the crystal skull wake up your innate knowing that we are all God. They purify you in divine fire, so that all within you is transmuted into the purest white love. Angels sing over you, cleansing the energy around you and lightening your heart. Some of these glorious angels return with you to your daily life and continue to sing over you. No matter what is going on around you, they are tuning you into Source love.

When you have undertaken this training course and passed any associated challenges, you are invited to become a member of the Brotherhood of the Golden Robe. Lord Kuthumi is a hierarch of this Brotherhood. He takes on the burdens of the world and transmutes them through his being. Dwjhal Khul, too, is a member of the Brotherhood of the Golden Robe, as are many of the great masters. There are also people incarnate on Earth who have become members in past lives and are still part of this august but modest body without being aware of it. They undertake this service with joy and receive much help from the angelic realms and the masters.

Visualization to Visit the Hall of Service with Joy

1. Prepare a space where you can be relaxed and undisturbed. Light a candle if you can.
2. Sit quietly and breathe comfortably into your heart centre, feeling yourself surrendering to the higher energy.
3. Focus upon your activated Earth Star.
4. Ask Archangel Michael to place his deep blue cloak of protection around you.
5. Step onto an escalator of deep yellow shimmering light and allow yourself to be taken up through the radiant cosmos to the Hall of Service with Joy.
6. Lord Kuthumi himself is standing at the entrance. He greets you lovingly and touches your heart centre until it is glowing white. Then he places a yellow robe over you.

7. The circular hall is filled with people and you sit down and make yourself comfortable.
8. You are aware of a great crystal skull emitting slow pulses of alternately golden yellow and golden orange light.
9. If you wish, you can place your personal etheric crystal skull on your third eye. Or you can allow the light to enter your third eye. It contains sacred geometric codes that are transmuting the old and waking you to the knowing of your God self and the God self of every sentient being. Relax.
10. Archangel Metatron stands behind you. Feel yourself lighting up like a golden orange beacon.
11. He is placing his hand on your third eye, over your personal crystal skull if it is there, holding and sealing all this light in your energy fields.
12. When you have received all that you need to today, Lord Kuthumi and Archangel Metatron ask you if you wish to be a member of the Brotherhood of the Golden Robe.
13. If you say no, you can relax and continue to bathe in the light. If you answer yes, they touch the yellow robe you are wearing until it glows a beautiful deep gold. Now you can truly serve with joy.
14. Thank Lord Kuthumi and Archangel Metatron and return down the escalator. If you are a member of the Brotherhood of the Golden Robe, you can see or sense your golden robe touching and transmuting problems throughout the world.
15. When you are ready, open your eyes, knowing you truly are a walking master.

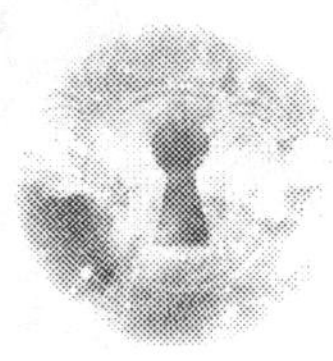

CHAPTER 28

Hall of Learning 10: Gateway to Other Dimensions

In the cycle of life, spring and the new Moon offer hope and new beginnings. The spiritual path is the same. At a certain point of your development, when you have finished a cycle, a glorious new door opens, allowing access to other dimensions.

In this Hall of Learning, information is downloaded to you about the elemental, angelic and unicorn kingdoms, so new worlds open up and you can connect at a much deeper level with the many beings in the higher dimensions.

Elemental and angelic beings, who come from the heart of God, are on an accelerated spiritual growth path. They have taken full advantage of the wondrous energies now focused on Earth and their growth has expanded accordingly. They are like a river in full spate rushing towards the ocean of love, while most humans are flowing alongside them on a parallel but slower course.

When you step through this special gateway, angels and Illumined Masters really influence you. Choices are presented to you, and you may fly along your current golden path or decide to move to a different path and explore the magic and mystery offered there.

Whichever you decide, everything speeds up. You enter this gateway as a caterpillar and emerge as a butterfly. An entirely new world of possibilities opens up for you.

When you enter this Hall of Learning, the teaching skull pours the gentlest, softest spring green light over you, downloading into your energy fields the keys and codes that help you to disengage from the old and embrace the new.

Here you understand the sacred geometric formations that enable a caterpillar to rest in its cocoon while an unbelievable transformation takes place, based on the sacred spiritual laws of trust and faith and the miraculous laws of alchemy. The caterpillar rests while it is overlaid with the higher-resonating template of the beautiful winged creature it is turning into. It emerges as a fifth-dimensional butterfly radiating the wisdom of Orion and acting as a true messenger for the angels.

If you are receptive to phenomenal change and have the courage to sign up for it, Lord Kuthumi will invite Archangels Gabriel and Christiel to touch your consciousness. Archangel Gabriel will cocoon you in his pure white light for a moment, wiping away the old and holding within your consciousness for a fraction of an instant the Light of Truth. He is offering you an ineffable gift: the most precious opportunity of metamorphosis. And at every level within you, change will take place.

You may find at this point that your physical body demands sleep. You may keep feeling tired or find that you are dozing off when you least expect it. This is because your spiritual and physical bodies have to align so that the changes taking place can be transferred to your consciousness.

Then Archangel Christiel will hold open your ineffable causal chakra while his lunar angels will sing in the connections that you can now make. At this point you may see or remember unicorns, angels, elementals, masters, dragons or other beings from different dimensions. You may sense yourself receiving Archangel Christiel's pure white light. Even if you do not see or feel anything, incredible shifts will be taking place in your auric fields as well as in the cells of your body. Know that your etheric wings have developed. Your divine blueprint has changed. Your new possibilities are endless. As you relax, you can soar above your life and see golden gates opening to you that were previously closed. Paths appear that you could not see before. Affirm that you are ready and know that all you need will be given to you.

In fact, being ready for the new is all that you need to do. Everything else will be done for and to you. It is beyond your control. Like the caterpillar, it is time for you to surrender. The embryonic butterfly trusts. Trust too. Let Archangel Gabriel hold you in his cocoon of light. Once you have experienced this, you will know that all things are possible. You will expect miracles and know that they are an everyday part of existence in the higher dimensions. And yet you will retain your sense of awe and wonder. This is vitally important, for it is this energy that allows the universe to open the golden gate for you.

Visualization to Visit the Gateway to Other Dimensions

1. Prepare a space where you can be relaxed and undisturbed. Light a candle if you can.
2. Sit quietly and breathe comfortably with the intention of visiting the Hall of Learning that offers the gateway to other dimensions.
3. Focus upon your activated Earth Star.
4. Ask Archangel Michael to place his deep blue cloak of protection around you.
5. A million angels surround you with magnificent light. They create a note beyond your auditory capacity. It propels you through the dimensions to the Hall of Learning wherein lies the great dimensional gateway.

6. You sit in the front row in front of the great teaching skull.
7. Soft leaf-green light pours into your mind and fills your aura, preparing you for change.
8. Lord Kuthumi touches you and it feels as if a great current is flowing through your entire being. You relax.
9. Archangel Gabriel places you in a cocoon of pure white light. Surrender totally as the old vanishes and a bright new light enters.
10. Archangel Christiel touches your causal chakra above your head. Sense your chakra opening like the glowing milky white Moon.
11. You may hear angels singing. You may be aware of elementals, angels, unicorns or great masters around you. Enjoy the impressions.
12. Sense your etheric wings expanding and your body metamorphosing into that of a cosmic being.
13. A vast golden gate swings open and you walk or fly through it. Stay open to the new world of possibilities you are entering.
14. Return to where you started, full of gratitude to Lord Kuthumi, Archangels Gabriel and Christiel and the expanded worlds.
15. Anticipate the new.

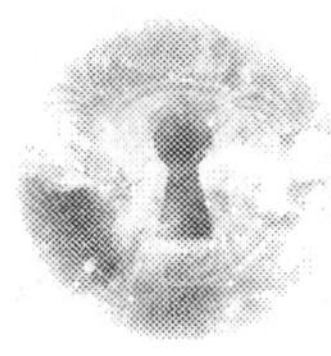

CHAPTER 29

Hall of Learning 11: The Divine Feminine

In the first Hall of Learning, you learn about basic balance and harmony. By the time you reach the eleventh hall, it is assumed that your 12 chakras are fully balanced, your masculine and feminine energy is in equilibrium and you are a walking master.

Many understand that the divine feminine qualities of caring, empathy, wisdom, healing, peace, love, kindness and nurturing are incredibly powerful. Each of these and many other feminine qualities can transform hard into soft, dissolve walls and open hearts in a way that masculine energies simply cannot. Only when the master has both feminine and masculine qualities in their armoury of tools are they allowed to access the deeper secrets of feminine wisdom. The ultimate secret of feminine wisdom is the secret of life itself.

In the sacred teaching schools of the past it was easier for females to take this initiation into the great mysteries of the universe. It was understood that women were entrusted with a womb, the dark cave in which new life grew in safety, and then produced milk, the perfect nourishment to enable the baby to flourish. Menstruation and birth were considered to be internal initiations, which was why women traditionally did not need external ones.

Now that men are balancing their 12 chakras and coming into masculine–feminine alignment, many of them are ready to enter this Hall of Learning too, having undergone the sacred initiations they need to prepare themselves for it.

In this 11th Hall of Learning we are given access to the deepest secrets of alchemy and divine light. These are held within the black yin energy.

Blackness is the absence of light and it is in this space that seeds alchemize and sprout, caterpillars transform into butterflies, a sperm is planted in the deep recesses of the female and a baby grows.

During sleep, when the conscious mind switches off, the deeper states of understanding can be accessed. In this space of hibernation, consciousness can transform. For example, if you are in the dark cave of sleep and a unicorn enters your dream, it is touching your soul essence and enabling you to undergo shifts as profound as that of the caterpillar becoming a butterfly. And while you are asleep, angels can sing over you, literally changing or healing your mental, emotional, physical or spiritual state.

The baby in the womb has its own soul blueprint and yet it can be influenced by external factors, especially the emotions of the mother. It is the same with seeds. Each is encrypted with its divine agenda to grow into a beautiful flower, tree or vegetable. Yet the quality of soil, the weather and thoughts of humans who tend the seeds affect the outcome.

Feminine wisdom understands this and provides the best conditions for the baby and the seed. All is a co-creation with Source.

The Magi, those hugely powerful priests and priestesses of Atlantis, understood the alchemy of feminine wisdom. It is the ability to awaken your vision with the breath of life.

Light contains spiritual information and knowledge. The growth of a new being in the dark is creation based on trust in and surrender to the Divine. The ability to connect the new essence to Source so that the spark of life is ignited is the divine feminine secret.

Breath is life. It is Source energy. The mighty Universal Angel Mary is the holder of this light frequency.

The Magi also knew it was within the cocoon of darkness that a soul could heal and grow. They would take a person who was out of balance, especially one who was mentally ill, out of their body into a black cocoon. Here they could sing them into divine harmony again or they could whisper to the soul and enable changes to take place. We can still do this. With intention and surrender in this Hall of Learning you can transform fear into love and imbalance into balance.

When enough people can transcend the limitations of the collective consciousness, we will be able regrow limbs and change DNA.

It is really important as we stand on the brink of the new Golden Age that as many pure masters as possible are entrusted with the divine codes of light that are downloaded in this Hall of Learning.

Those who study here are bathed in transparent aquamarine and are given permanent access to the wisdom of Orion, the love of the Cosmic Heart and the Halls of Amenti. All provide examples of the working of the divine feminine.

The masters and angels of Orion hold wisdom for this universe. This is beyond knowledge – it is the understanding of how to use knowledge for the highest good. When enough souls hold the wisdom blueprint for the universe within their energy fields, the people of this planet will automatically do what is for the highest good of all.

The Cosmic Heart is in a sense a womb. It receives pure love from Source that regenerates those who enter it and transforms lower energies into transcendent love.

The Halls of Amenti hold great knowledge. When you access it, this automatically ensures that you have the power to use the knowledge with wisdom.

The transformation of hurt into loving wisdom is divine feminine magic. Understanding this opens doors to higher enlightenment.

Visualization to Visit the Hall of the Secrets of Divine Feminine Wisdom

1. Prepare a space where you can be relaxed and undisturbed. Light a candle if you can.
2. Sit quietly and breathe comfortably with the intention of visiting the hall where the secrets of divine feminine wisdom are found.
3. Focus upon your activated Earth Star.
4. Ask Archangel Michael to place his deep blue cloak of protection around you.
5. A golden escalator is appearing in front of you. You step onto it and glide smoothly up through the dimensions, through the dark tunnel that takes you to the hall.
6. The light is dim, but you can make out Lord Kuthumi waiting for you. He leads you to a seat and asks you what aspect of yourself you wish to change. Relax.
7. Here the Angel Mary bathes you in pale, translucent, aquamarine light filled with the sacred geometric codes triggered by your stated wish. Hold your intention.
8. The light gradually fades until you find yourself in a cocoon of darkness. Breathe comfortably and surrender. In no-thought comes change. You are beyond time.

9. Slowly, translucent aquamarine light filters into your cocoon. Stretch and sense the cocoon breaking open.
10. A change has taken place in your soul. You may not be aware of it for some time. Just trust.
11. Lord Kuthumi reaches out a hand and leads you to your golden escalator.
12. Thank him and allow yourself to glide down to waking reality.

CHAPTER 30

Hall of Learning 12: Your Ninth-Dimensional Cosmic Master Light

Only those who are at the upper levels of the fifth dimension can gain access to this particular Hall of Learning, but remember that many people are now reaching this level without giving themselves credit for it. We tend to see our faults and mistakes, while the angels see us from a higher perspective. They see our light and our magnificence. So, don't underestimate your spiritual light. Be prepared to knock on the door to this hall before you go to sleep or into meditation and ask for entry!

The light in this facility is diamond bright, for this is a ninth-dimensional teaching space. Here we are primed to understand and accept ninth-dimensional energies. The ninth-dimensional blueprints are almost unbelievably light, with totally symmetrical geometrical formations that impact perfectly and positively on our consciousness.

Remember high frequencies consume lower ones, so the service we can offer the world increases hugely when we enter this temple of learning, for we carry its light back in our aura.

In this hall you will be linked directly to Lakumay, the ascended ninth-dimensional aspect of Sirius. Here the Christ Light is stored at a ninth-dimensional frequency in a golden tetrahedron surrounded by a complete rainbow circle. The Christ Light is the golden aspect of pure Source agape that protects, heals and transmutes all into love. As you are bathed in Christ Light, the keys and codes of the spiritual technology of the future light up, matching ones that lie dormant in your energetic fields, so that you can utilize them. As you absorb the vibration of the Gold Ray of Christ into your cellular structure, you radiate it to others, lighting them up, opening their hearts and expanding their minds.

The Pleiades is a seventh-dimensional star cluster, but it holds a ninth-dimensional healing key. In this Hall of Learning you will be plugged directly into this radiant ninth-dimensional aspect of the Pleiades. Here you can receive a direct download of Source love and healing through the blue cosmic rose. This opens and heals your lower heart then lights up the higher transcendent chambers and allows you to spread Pleiadean heart healing on to others. The archangels of the Pleiades will link into you and help you.

You will also connect to the ninth-dimensional aspect of the Christed Mahatma. The Mahatma energy is a pool to which the highest frequency beings of Golden Atlantis added their vital force. As a result, when you invoke it, this energy offers you accelerated ascension. It connects you to much higher aspects of your soul energy.

When you access the golden-white vibration of the Christed Mahatma in this hall, you will learn to add the light of your own personal ninth-dimensional cosmic master aspect to the original pool of light. By drawing the Mahatma through you into the Earth and to those around you, then back into the pool so that others can draw on it, you can massively impact your own ascension as well as that of the planet.

Lord Kuthumi will introduce you to the masters of Orion, who will show you the ninth-dimensional wisdom blueprint for the universe. The joy, peace, love and bliss of this is currently beyond our comprehension. Nevertheless, as this plan and vision for our future is laid over your consciousness, openings and possibilities are sparked. It is the equivalent of living in a small cottage and having an architect with an enlightened, expanded viewpoint laying the plan for a magnificent house over the original plans for your home. Somewhere in your mind you start to see new potential and wonderful possibilities open up.

You will also meet the masters of Neptune, who hold the ninth-dimensional spiritual light for the universe. As you tune into them, they will download as much of this light into you as you can hold. This is a fast track to enlightenment, as you will see the world from a higher perspective. Eventually, you will view life with universal wisdom.

Ninth-dimensional pure white unicorns will honour you with a ninth-dimensional blessing that will pour from their majestic golden horns to expand your enlightenment and open you to higher mastery.

Archangels Zadkiel and Gabriel will hold you in the ninth-dimensional aspect of the Cosmic Diamond Violet Flame. Archangel Zadkiel's violet energies will consume any dense energy within your cellular structure and transmute them into pure light. The shining facets of Archangel Gabriel's cosmic diamond will clarify, illuminate and purify you. As the vast sacred diamond is placed over you, it will expand your levels of enlightenment and fill you with joy.

Archangel Metatron will pour ninth-dimensional ascension light through you. As soon as your Stellar Gateway is fully open and spinning at the higher fifth-dimensional frequency, he draws down ninth-dimensional Source light and bathes you in it. This happens at those moments when you are divinely prepared and ready to access it.

The great Universal Angel Mary is also ready and willing to pour her aquamarine light through you at a ninth-dimensional frequency so that you experience her incredible love, compassion and purity of heart. As she does this, she places her vast feathery wings around you and cocoons you in divine bliss.

There are many universal angels who will give you a ninth-dimensional transfusion of their particular ray if you are ready to receive it. These angelic beings work throughout the universes and we call them archangels for simplicity, but they live on the ninth-dimensional frequencies. All the angels in charge of the fifth-dimensional chakras are universal angels who are focusing on Earth right now to help us prepare for the new Golden Age:

- The pure white Universal Angel Butyalil will help you see your divine magnificence and flow with the great currents of your life.
- The Universal Angel Sandalphon will pour silver light through you to help you ground yourself fully into the heart of Lady Gaia.
- The Universal Angel Roquiel will pour his black energy through you to enable you to work more powerfully with the ley lines and help to build the crystalline grid round the planet.
- The Universal Angel Uriel will pour his deep gold light through you to help you bring back your deepest wisdom.
- The Universal Angel Chamuel will pour his pink white light through you to illuminate your heart.

- The Universal Angel Michael will pour his deep royal blue light through you to expand your strength and cosmic communications.
- The Universal Angel Raphael will pour his crystal emerald light through you to expand your enlightenment.
- The Universal Angel Jophiel will pour his crystal gold light through you to link you to higher energies in the universe.
- The Universal Angel Christiel will pour his golden milk-white light through you to light up your connections with the higher masters, angels and beings of light.
- The Universal Angel Mariel will pour his magenta light through you to bring forwards the faster frequencies of your soul.

Many of the great Illumined Masters carry ninth-dimensional light in their energy fields. You can also call on them to overlight you and ignite the keys and codes of your ninth-dimensional master self.

As a graduate of the 12 Halls of Learning under the supervision of Lord Kuthumi, you will become an enlightened ascended master and your light will profoundly affect others on Earth and help the ascension of the planet.

Visualization to Visit the Ninth-Dimensional Hall of Learning

1. Prepare a space where you can relax and be undisturbed.
2. Light a candle and dedicate it to higher enlightenment and ascension.
3. Sit quietly and breathe comfortably with the intention of visiting Lord Kuthumi's ninth-dimensional Hall of Learning.
4. Focus upon your activated Earth Star.
5. Ask Archangel Michael to place his deep blue cloak of protection around you.
6. Imagine or sense your essence opening like a rose, ready to be bathed in ninth-dimensional light.
7. Invoke the ninth-dimensional Christ Light held within Lakumay and sense the golden love pouring into you. Relax and bathe in it, then spread it.
8. Invoke the ninth-dimensional healing light of the blue cosmic Pleiadean rose to pour into you. Relax and bathe in it, then spread it.
9. Invoke the ninth-dimensional Christed Mahatma to flow through you as golden-white light. Relax and bathe in it, then spread it to others. Send your own ninth-dimensional cosmic master light back into the pool.
10. Invoke the masters of the ninth-dimensional aspect of Orion to place the wisdom blueprint for the universe over your soul blueprint. Relax and absorb it.
11. Invoke the masters of the ninth-dimensional aspect of Neptune to drench you in the spiritual light of the universe. Relax and bathe in it.
12. Invoke the ninth-dimensional Cosmic Diamond Violet Flame to be placed over you to expand your enlightenment and fill you with cosmic joy. Relax and bathe in it, then spread it.
13. Invoke the great Universal Angel Metatron to bathe you in ninth-dimensional ascension light from Source. Relax and receive it, then spread it.
14. Invoke the ninth-dimensional pure white unicorns to pour a blessing of enlightenment and mastery over you.

15. Invoke the great Universal Angel Mary to pour her aquamarine light through you at a ninth-dimensional frequency to experience her incredible love, compassion and purity of heart. Feel her feathery wings around you, cocooning you in divine bliss.
16. Invoke Universal Angel Butyalil to pour his pure white ninth-dimensional light through you to help you see your divine magnificence and flow with the great currents of your life.
17. Invoke Universal Angel Sandalphon to pour ninth-dimensional silver light through you to help you ground yourself fully into the heart of Lady Gaia.
18. Invoke Universal Angel Roquiel to pour his ninth-dimensional black energy through you to enable you to work more powerfully with the ley lines and help to build the crystalline grid round the planet.
19. Invoke Universal Angel Uriel to pour his ninth-dimensional deep gold light through you to help you bring back your deepest wisdom.
20. Invoke Universal Angel Chamuel to pour his ninth-dimensional pink-white light through you to illuminate your heart.
21. Invoke Universal Angel Michael to pour his ninth-dimensional deep royal blue light through you to expand your strength and cosmic communications.
22. Invoke Universal Angel Raphael to pour his ninth-dimensional crystal emerald light through you to expand your enlightenment.
23. Invoke Universal Angel Jophiel to pour his ninth-dimensional crystal gold light through you to link you to higher energies in the universe.
24. Invoke Universal Angel Christiel to pour his ninth-dimensional golden milk-white light through you to light up your connections with the higher masters, angels and beings of light.
25. Invoke Universal Angel Mariel to pour his ninth-dimensional magenta light through you to bring forwards the faster frequencies of your soul.
26. Note how your energy fields have lit up and expanded.
27. Thank Lord Kuthumi and return to waking consciousness, knowing an aspect of you is a ninth-dimensional walking master.

The Great Masters and Their Lessons

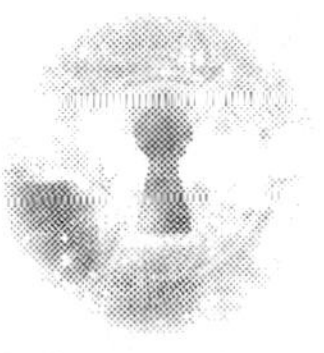

CHAPTER 31

Become an Intergalactic Master

Your original divine spark from Source is your monad, which is 12th-dimensional. Each one of us is part of an ineffable monad. Your monad sends out aspects of itself into the cosmos to learn and experience. These are known as soul aspects. You are part of your soul or Higher Self and the aim of enlightenment is to see everything from the wider and higher perspective of your soul. It is rather like a grandparent whose children scatter round the world and raise their own children and grandchildren. However, they are all connected to the original family, even though they think they have lost touch. And all have a longing for a reunion with their wise grandparents.

In one way we are as insignificant as a leaf on a tree. In another we are unique and incredibly important. The entire universal system would be different if we weren't who we are!

We live in one of many vast interconnected multi-dimensional universes. Although we have had learnings on many planets and in many galaxies, cosmic spaces and etheric realities, our current involvement is on Earth. We bring with us to this life the knowledge, wisdom and light that we need for this experience. Much more understanding is held in our soul and we can retrieve it when we are ready. As we become enlightened masters, we access more of this light.

When we reach mastery, we have more opportunities to serve. One of these is to train to become an intergalactic master. Then we operate at a soul level during sleep to serve the universe. A team of masters works for the Intergalactic Council to maintain balance and harmony throughout the universes.

Many people currently in incarnation have been to Earth several times during their soul expansion. While it is considered to be a very difficult training ground, this planet also engenders feelings of love, loyalty and a desire to serve. A great number of people who love, honour and respect our planet are serving as ambassadors for Earth or even intergalactic masters on the inner planes.

You may desire to train to become an intergalactic master or you may already be one without realizing it, for the work is done on an unconscious level so it is not possible to judge anyone else's life. The person who is always tired or sick or never seems to accomplish much in life may be doing incredible soul work out of their body. Their spirit may be travelling every night while they are asleep or during the day during their daydreams, doing wonderful healing or rescue or intergalactic work.

You can only become an intergalactic messenger, negotiator, advisor or worker when your 12 fifth-dimensional chakras are fully active and you are ready to serve. Many of us undertook these intergalactic roles during incarnations in the Golden Era of Atlantis. Now is awakening time. It is time to reactivate the keys and codes in our energy fields. If you feel the energetic pull, it may be the moment to sign on for a revision course.

Intergalactic Mastery

Commander Ashtar and Seraphina, the mighty Seraphim, train beings in 12 intergalactic schools to serve as ambassadors for Earth. Invoke Commander Ashtar, and if it is the right path for you, he will issue you with an invitation to attend these schools. This invitation will be lodged in your energy fields and you may accept it now or at a later date.

Commander Ashtar works closely with Master Marko, who was a great one in Atlantis and later became head of the Inca civilization. He is a representative of the highest galactic confederation of our solar system.

The capital of our solar system is on Saturn. It is run by the Council of Nine, an advanced group consciousness. During the Golden Era of Atlantis the High Priests and Priestesses would attend special meetings there, accessing Saturn in their spirit bodies via the etheric highways from the Great Crystal of Atlantis.

Another mighty master who can assist you in intergalactic mastery is Lord Hilarion, a member of the Intergalactic Council who works closely with Commander Ashtar and Master Marko. He is currently the negotiator for Earth on the Council of Saturn.

There are thousands of great beings working throughout the universe, but we would specially like to mention Serapis Bey, the great High Priest of Atlantis who carried the White Flame of Atlantis, because he is so well known. After the fall of Atlantis he worked in his spirit body with Archangel Metatron and Thoth to build the Great Pyramid of Egypt. This cosmic pyramid is linked energetically to Sirius and Orion and the knowledge and wisdom of these stars and galaxies comes through galactic pathways to it. The keys and codes of universal wisdom are held there. It is a vast cosmic computer. For example, Thoth and Serapis Bey programmed it to activate the kundalini of the planet, which is held in the Earth Star in London, so that it rose at the Cosmic Moment of 11.11 a.m. on 21 December, 2012. And at the same time the 33 cosmic portals bringing in Christ Light were set to open.

Seraphina's intergalactic school doesn't just deal with our local area of Earth. The training covers different star systems, too, and when you participate, you receive a real sense of being an enlightened child of the universes.

So, if you have a passionate love for Earth and a desire to protect her, you may like to channel some of your energy into becoming an intergalactic master.

One of the first steps in your intergalactic mastery process is to learn how to link your chakras to the equivalent stars, as the stars, planets and galaxies are the sacred chakras of the universe. Many people are currently practising this. It is so important that we both teach it in our seminars and via CDs and downloads.

When you link your chakras to the stars, you start to download the knowledge, wisdom and light held within them into your own chakra system. Because fingers of light are reaching out into the universe and bringing back pure light, your aura becomes stronger, clearer and brighter.

When your fifth-dimensional chakras are plugged into the celestial bodies that are vibrating at the seventh-dimensional frequency, your energy system is flooded with light, which has to be absorbed and integrated. You may need to rest to allow this to happen.

If you deeply love this planet and want to serve in a universal capacity, it may help to meet some of the intergalactic masters and absorb their energy. Archangel Butyalil, the pure white angel who is in charge of the flow of the cosmic currents and ensures they are in cosmic harmony, will take you to Seraphina's training school when you ask.

Visualization to Meet the Intergalactic Masters

1. Prepare a space where you can be relaxed and undisturbed.
2. Sit quietly and breathe comfortably with the intention of meeting intergalactic masters who can help you.
3. Focus upon your activated Earth Star.
4. Ask Archangel Michael to place his deep blue cloak of protection around you.
5. Light a candle and dedicate it to being in service.
6. Be aware of a pure white flame approaching you. Out of it steps Serapis Bey. He stands in front of you, looking into your eyes, and you may be aware of light flowing into your mind.
7. And now a dazzling golden light is shining on you and you are aware that Commander Ashtar is smiling at you as he awakens your past service memories. This may only last for a fraction of a second, but it will help you to take important decisions.
8. Lord Hilarion arrives in a flash of orange light. He touches your third eye chakra and the higher possibilities held within your divine blueprint are illuminated for a moment.
9. Lastly, Master Marko stands in front of you in a star-spangled green and purple cloak. He reaches towards you and his light enters your heart.
10. Thank the masters before they leave.
11. Your aura is expanding now to encompass the Earth. Then it reaches out to the universe.
12. A door appears in front of you marked 'Intergalactic Training'. If you wish to, you may push it open.
13. A pure white dazzling light fills the space. Archangel Butyalil awaits your decision.

14. If you wish to go with him to Seraphina's training school, he will take you in your sleep tonight. Use your day to raise your frequency so that you are ready for this most awesome spiritual advancement.

CHAPTER 32

Walk in the Steps of the Illumined Ones

Enlightenment entails being aware of everything from a higher and wider perspective, witnessing without judgement. Metaphorically, when you are an enlightened master you stand at the top of a mountain with your crown, third eye and heart chakras open and observe the whole picture of your life and those of others spread below you.

Your open crown chakra signifies that you are standing in your power and majesty, you are in command of the situation and you are receiving higher energy and wisdom from the vast universe. You must ground this. Spiritually, you are a king/queen or emperor/empress.

Your third eye is now a highly polished crystal ball. You see with clarity, for all the veils of illusion have been dissolved. It is as if you are looking through a very clean window with the curtains pulled back. You can see through the mists of human misconception to the divine light beyond, where there is only love. You don't have to physically see this, you just have to know it is there.

Your heart chakra is fully open, with the 33 petals shimmering white. As an enlightened master, you never hold onto dense emotions in your heart because you can see and feel the truth, which is that everything is done in a search for love or as part of a pre-life soul agreement to serve. Therefore there is no judgement and nothing to be hurt about.

Because of this, the blueprint for the upper fifth-dimensional enlightened master is total health and tranquillity.

At this time of special spiritual advancement, we are all being presented with the opportunity to attain this goal. All those who wish to become walking masters in this lifetime can now follow in the footsteps of the great Illumined Ones. They have blazed a trail in front of us and are waiting to embrace and help us. When we read about them, talk about them and tune into them, their light touches us and propels us forwards. And when we ourselves are walking masters, we in turn help others on their way.

All of the mighty beings we are following were trained through lifetimes for the tasks they undertook. They want you to remember that you, too, have been prepared both in physical bodies and on the inner planes for this special and unprecedented lifetime. Do not underestimate the power of the planning that has gone into your life. Take up the challenge and live an extraordinary life. It will affect your entire soul journey to mastery and enlightenment and you may influence hundreds or thousands of people.

Here are some of the Illumined Ones who are ready to help you now.

Master Lanto

Master Lanto is one of the most loving of the Illumined Masters to have walked the planet. A golden yellow-pink light flows from his love-filled mind. Even more wonderful is that his heart centre was so highly developed when he was on Earth that people could see the light from his heart shining through his skin.

He has now agreed to be the master of the Second Ray of Wisdom and Illumination, a role for which he is vastly overqualified, but his enormous charisma will enable the light of this ray to accelerate everyone's mastery and enlightenment.

Like St Germain, who was also the Mage Merlin, Lanto is a master of alchemy, meaning that he can turn light into physical manifestations.

His retreat is above the Teton mountains of Wyoming, USA, and he was the master of the Council of the Royal Teton Retreat. (He was succeeded by the ascended master Confucius.) This is also where the Great White Brotherhood meets. He placed a Golden Flame of Illumination containing the Christ Light above these mountains to influence all those who are ready to receive his wisdom. He also anchored a Golden Flame of Illumination in China, in the retreat of the Archangels Jophiel and Christine, to support the Chinese people.

In his past lives he was the Yellow Emperor, a benevolent ruler who introduced systems of government, law, music and arts to China, and supported Taoism. Fifteen hundred years later he incarnated as the Duke of Zhou, a ruler in China. Again, he was a wise one who lead by example and believed in ruling in harmony with Heaven.

In all his lives he studied and practised the way of wisdom and love. We on Earth are able to tune into him and benefit from his extraordinary light.

Visualization to Meet Master Lanto

1. Find a place where you can be quiet and undisturbed.
2. Imagine it is a hot day and you are standing under a pure, shimmering white waterfall.
3. Step out feeling cleansed and purified. Stand in the glorious hot Sun and dry out.
4. Be aware of the incredible Master Lanto approaching, his aura shimmering yellow and pink, with pink light blazing from his heart centre.
5. As he approaches you can feel his golden wisdom and all-encompassing love flowing over and through you. Immerse yourself in his energy and relax.
6. Master Lanto is smiling at you as he invites you to travel with him to the Teton mountains.
7. You go with him to the mountains and stand together in the Golden Flame of Illumination.
8. Then he gradually withdraws and disappears, leaving your aura blazing gold and pink.

Babaji

Babaji simply means 'revered father'. He is a Mahavatar, which means 'a great avatar', and indeed is one of the great avatars of all time. He is known as the deathless avatar because he has served humanity for thousands of years, having transcended death. He can appear and disappear or make himself invisible at will.

Babaji is in permanent communion and communication with the Christ. They work together for the betterment of the world.

He also follows the progress of individuals as well as humanity. Diana was once sent a photograph of a *tai chi* class with a magnificent shining Orb over it containing the spirit of Babaji watching the class. On another occasion, when a yoga class was taking place in her house, an Orb appeared over the teacher, again containing the spirit of Babaji and this time observing and assessing the yoga teacher's spiritual progress.

As she was relaxing in her armchair contemplating whom to write about in this chapter, Diana thought of Babaji, and no sooner had that happened than he appeared, floating at head height in a magnificent transparent ball of light. This felt so peaceful and normal that she felt no awe, just delight. Typically, all the great spiritual questions she could have asked vanished from her mind and she asked about the bubble he was travelling in. Was it a high-frequency Orb? He reminded her that every being who has ever incarnated must travel with an angel, in case their human compassion disturbs the balance of their karma. This is why even the greatest masters are seen within an angelic Orb. In Babaji's case, the Orb was his guardian angel. Because our angels advance spiritually and raise their frequency as we do, Babaji's was like a Seraphim, shimmering with incredible luminosity. Also, it was totally clear, indicating that the angelic being was using its active masculine energy, rather than its milky, opaque, passive, feminine light. Apparently, this was to protect Babaji from the lower frequency of humans. He vibrates at a 12th-dimensional frequency.

That night Babaji floated in again and this time invited Diana to travel with him. Instantly her spirit was in his Orb, sitting beside him. They travelled to the Himalayas and floated high over the mountains together while he showed her the ascended world and the glorious future we are all aiming for. Everything seemed possible!

The wonderful thing was that for the next few days Babaji's energy could be felt in her house, not just by Diana herself, but also by Tim when he visited.

Reading about Babaji or calling on him automatically draws a spiritual blessing to you. For an instant you are touched by 12th-dimensional energy beyond your comprehension. It dramatically advances your journey to enlightened mastery.

Visualization to Meet Babaji

1. Find a place where you can be quiet and undisturbed.
2. A big translucent bubble is floating towards you. In it, sitting cross-legged, is the illustrious Babaji.
3. As the ball of light reaches you, it opens, and you find yourself inside it, sitting beside Babaji.
4. You feel his incredible peace and radiant joy as you glide through the clear blue air over the Himalayan mountains.
5. You may hear the Seraphim singing.
6. For a fraction of a second you see the world with Babaji's 12th-dimensional vision. Breathe deeply as this unconsciously lights you up.
7. The Sun rises over the mountains, heralding a new world, as you float with Babaji back to where you started.
8. The deathless Avatar Babaji leaves you with some guiding thoughts before he disappears.
9. Send thanks to the Mahavatar Babaji.
10. Open your eyes, knowing you have activated your inner keys to enlightenment and mastery.

Master Josiah

Josiah is a lesser-known Illumined One, but nevertheless he has much to teach us. He comes from Sirius and is now the Lord of Karma for the Ninth Ray.

He was once the king of Judah. When he was eight years old, his father, Amon, was murdered, leaving him without a strong masculine influence and a protector. However, this strengthened Josiah and later he instituted religious reforms that brought purity and goodness into the church.

In another life, he incarnated in Pompeii. When the city was destroyed by a volcano, he died in the cataclysm. He remained calm and collected, knew exactly what to do and worked with Archangel Uriel, the angel of peace and wisdom, as a bridge to help others with the transition. As a result of his selfless actions, some of those who passed ascended, and many were greatly helped.

When Diana was first given this information by her guide Kumeka for *Ascension Through Orbs*, she was bowled over. It made an enormous impact on her. Even now she asks that when she dies her spirit may act as a bridge to help others to pass. It seems such a beautiful act of service to help others until the very last minute of your life.

Josiah still helps with the consequences of volcanoes and earthquakes. If you are involved in such a problem or hear or see one on the news, ask him and his team of lightworkers to help. He brings transcendent love to wherever he is.

Visualization to Meet Master Josiah

1. Find a place where you can be quiet. Light a candle if you wish to.
2. See your Earth Star chakra as a great silver ball below you, grounding you.
3. Ask Archangel Gabriel to place his great diamond of purity and protection over you and sense yourself sitting in it.
4. Be aware of the mighty Master Josiah standing in front of you. He holds out his hand and you take it.
5. You follow him to a great spiritual mountain. At its foot, thousands of frightened souls are clamouring for help.
6. You and Master Josiah walk among them, spreading peace and calm.
7. The beautiful, wise, golden Archangel Uriel works with you.
8. Then your spirits create a vast bridge and all those souls pass over you to the higher realms.
9. You stare in wonder at the result of your act of service.
10. Master Josiah thanks you and reminds you to hold the intention of service whenever you can.
11. Archangel Uriel places golden light in your aura.

Peter the Great

After many incarnations in the nobility, Peter the Great became the Emperor of Russia in the seventeenth and eighteenth centuries. He undertook extensive reforms for the betterment of Russia and wanted to establish the country as a great nation. Like most great masters, he faced opposition to the changes, but he overcame these and he ascended after that lifetime.

In that life, he loved nature and animals, and he now oversees environmental and conservation movements. He works with Archangel Fhelyai, the angel of animals, to enable people to understand what special spiritual beings these creatures are. In this way, he helps to shift the consciousness of humanity towards animals. And when polluters of the planets die, he and Archangel Purlimiek, the angel of nature, work with them to help them understand the impact of what they have done.

During one of the early experiments of Atlantis the continent was overrun with huge animals – giant elephants, mammoths, massive birds, cats, horses and many other creatures – who became very aggressive. Life on the surface became almost impossible and when all peaceful methods to control them failed, a five-nation conference was organized to discuss the situation. Delegates teleported from Russia, the Sudan, India and Peru to Atlantis. Finally, in 52000BCE, they detonated nuclear bombs underground, hoping that this would kill the beasts. The repercussions of this event did cause the creatures to perish, but eventually all the people perished too. As a consequence, 2,000 years later, the Earth shifted on its axis and Atlantis eventually became five islands.

The fallout of those nuclear explosions still contaminates the Earth, and Peter the Great is still involved with cleansing and healing it at a deep level.

He is now the Lord of Karma for the 11th Ray and is helping to bring peace and healing to the planet.

VISUALIZATION TO MEET PETER THE GREAT

1. Find a place where you can be quiet and still. Light a candle if you can.
2. Let your roots go down into the heart of Lady Gaia.
3. Bring down the Gold Ray of Christ for your total protection, by saying:

   'I, [name], invoke the Gold Ray of Christ.'

4. You are aware of a hall full of people listening to a lecture on environmental issues.
5. Behind the lecturer stands Peter the Great, trying to influence them to help the planet.
6. Master Peter sees you and calls you. He asks you to hold a vision of the Earth as clear, beautiful and unpolluted.
7. Archangel Fhelyai, the glorious yellow angel of animals, is standing beside you. Send out his yellow light to touch the minds of the people and enable them to see the truly beautiful souls of animals.
8. Now Master Peter travels with you to show you a deep pit that reaches into the centre of the Earth. It is filled with radioactive material from the bombs set off in Atlantis.
9. Together you pour pure white light into it.
10. Master Peter puts his hand on your shoulder and thanks you for your service work.
11. He asks you to work with him again to help his mission and to accelerate your path to mastery.

CHAPTER 33

Lord Voosloo

The Illumined Being Lord Voosloo is a Universal Ascended Master and Lord of Light who vibrates at the 11th-dimensional frequency and comes from another universe. Originally entering this one through Helios, the Great Central Sun, he steps his frequency down through Neptune, the planet of higher spiritual awareness.

He has helped Earth at critical times when there has been a quantum shift in consciousness on the planet. He was a wise one in the time of Mu, a fourth-dimensional non-physical Golden Age on Earth, and assisted the beings of that time to ascend to the fifth dimension. By then he had helped them to learn what they had come to experience and so they returned to the inner planes.

This glorious ascended master also assisted the Earth at the time of the Golden Era of Atlantis. Those who responded to the clarion call to take part in the final experiment of Atlantis came from all over the universes. The 144,000 volunteers who were chosen to participate all vibrated in the upper spectrum of the fifth dimension. The first 12 High Priests and Priestesses of the Golden Age enabled these souls to understand Earth and helped them to maintain their frequency.

As the Golden Era reached the pinnacle of its evolution, new High Priests and Priestesses were invited who could prepare the people to bring forwards the gifts and powers that had already been encoded into them, especially the ability to use crystal technology. At this point Lord Voosloo came in to oversee the next step. The highest-frequency being ever to incarnate as a High Priest, he carried within his energy fields the keys and codes that lit up the complete fifth-dimensional crystalline blueprints of these Atlanteans and enabled the leap in consciousness that brought forwards the full greatness of the Golden Era of Atlantis.

Because our extraordinary planet is currently going through an unprecedented double-dimensional shift, the mighty Lord Voosloo is here again, this time specifically to help our ascension.

During his soul's journey he mastered all the frequencies of the Ninth Ray, the glorious Yellow Ray of Harmony and Perfect Balance. In fact, during Atlantis, he mastered equilibrium and the balance of masculine and feminine energies to such an extent that he became androgynous. He brought the Ninth Ray back to the planet in 2001 and he has not taken a physical body but has become the Chohan of this ray.

This very high-frequency ray is a beautiful warm sunshine yellow. It bathes those who can access it in joy and a desire to bring about harmony in themselves and on the planet. Its vibration triggers co-operation, togetherness, peace, aspiration and perfect balance. By pouring this sunshine yellow energy into the minds, chakras and energy fields of individuals and group souls who are ready, Lord Voosloo is working assiduously to prepare the consciousness of humanity for the new Golden Age. His vision is to help us all to make a smooth transition into higher realms.

Sunshine yellow is a colour of happiness, and by absorbing this frequency we are able to experience true joy, contentment, grace and bliss, as they did in the Golden Era of Atlantis. In addition, our aspiration to fly along on our golden ascension journey is enhanced. When lightworkers radiate this yellow light in their auras, it enables them to stand out as beacons of truth and wisdom for the new Golden Age.

Through this yellow ray, Lord Voosloo not only helps us understand the greatest wisdom of Golden Atlantis, he also heals the deepest wounds of our soul. He strengthens and balances any keys, codes and sacred geometry in our blueprint and our cells that have been distorted by lower frequencies. This enables divine perfection and perfect health to be established in our energetic matrix.

This ray is one of those that lights up and unifies our 12 chakras. As these become balanced and active, our 12 strands of DNA start to reconnect, and this is happening to more and more people as they become fifth-dimensional. In addition, since 2012 more babies are being born with their 12 strands of DNA already connected. These strands are inert until they are activated, but the sunshine energy of the Ninth Ray directed by Lord Voosloo is helping to reactivate them. You can also ask the unicorns and the Cosmic Diamond Violet Flame to keep the energy clear, high and blessed around those who are ready for the reactivation of their 12 strands of DNA. As this happens, more miracles will occur.

The Ninth Ray also helps to fully activate our fifth-dimensional blueprint. It lights up all the keys and codes of our glorious divine potential, and if we are ready, it enables us to participate in the adventure of the new Golden Age in an amazing way. By merging with the light of the great Lord Voosloo, we can experience Heaven on Earth.

For 10,000 years humans and most other beings on Earth have been carbon-based, so their chakras have spun slowly and have accepted and emitted only dim light. Trees, flowers, many animals and humans and some insects are now establishing their fifth-dimensional blueprint. The fifth-dimensional 12-chakra column is descending and anchoring in them, and as this happens, their structure is becoming crystalline rather than carbon, so that they can contain and radiate much more light.

A process is taking place on Earth that accelerates this transformation. Archangel Metatron and Lord Voosloo are placing fourth and fifth-dimensional crystalline energy round third-dimensional beings so that when they wake up, they can light up in an instant. In this way, millions of humans will be illuminated suddenly and be ready to take their place in the new Golden Age.

The Earth has been designed so that we can access two dimensions higher than our own frequency. When we are third-dimensional, we can connect to the fifth dimension and occasionally to the seventh dimension angelic realms. So a third-dimensional person may have times of open-heartedness, generosity, true co-operation and selflessness, but will revert to their familiar patterns. A fifth-dimensional person can connect on a much more constant basis to the seventh-dimensional angels and masters. In addition, they can link into the awesome and almost incomprehensibly light and joy-filled ninth dimension.

Because of this, ever since the Cosmic Moment in 2012 ninth-dimensional energies have been available to us on Earth. Some of these are the blue cosmic rose of the Pleiades, the Cosmic Diamond Violet Flame, the Christed Mahatma, the Gold Ray of Christ, the Cosmic Heart, the Instant Sun, the ninth-dimensional unicorns and the light of the masters of Orion.

Before Earth started to rise in frequency, the great masters and angels were creating a seventh-dimensional grid round the planet to shine higher light onto us in preparation for the ascension of the planet to the fifth dimension. Now Lord Voosloo and Archangel Metatron are leading a team of evolved beings in creating a ninth-dimensional grid round Earth. When you work with Lord Voosloo, you may be invited to be part of this team.

The Etheric Retreat of Lord Voosloo

The etheric retreat of Lord Voosloo is above Stonehenge, which is one of the most ancient and powerful portals on Earth. It is one of only four two-way inter-dimensional portals in the world. It is an anchor point on Earth for the sacred geometry of the ninth-dimensional grid connecting all the points of our universe at a very high frequency.

For thousands of years it has been closed and it is still only partially open. It is expected to be fully open by 2032. Nevertheless, if you visit it in your meditations or sleep, it will take you into your seventh-dimensional light body. At this level, you see through angelic eyes; in other words, you see the divine perfection in every person and situation. You are aware of the soul agreements behind many challenging circumstances. You see the shimmering ball of peace, love and harmony hovering over all the communities in the world. With enlightened eyes, you are aware that it is just waiting for the people in those communities to wake up and see with different eyes, so that it can bathe them in its luminous energies.

Diana had a beautiful experience when she visited Lord Voosloo's retreat with a party of high-frequency teachers from the Diana Cooper Foundation.

Only 22 people were allowed into the sacred centre of the stones at a time, so the rest of the party stood beyond the ropes and tuned in. They formed a circle and Diana deliberately stood with her back to the dawn light so that the others would see the Sun as it sailed over the horizon.

They created an ascension lift and together they visited the seventh-dimensional chamber above Stonehenge, then moved up to the ninth-dimensional etheric retreat of Lord Voosloo, where he awaited them with radiant joy. As this happened, the Sun must have risen, for Diana could feel it on her back and in her inner eyes as if it was holding her in extraordinary sunshine yellow light. It was an ineffable feeling.

Lord Voosloo, Archangel Metatron and Uriel worked with the group until Diana could feel the yellow ray shimmering and scintillating round her. Ninth-dimensional energies poured in and instantly the yellow-gold light spread out from them around the universe, connecting every star, planet, galaxy and form of sacred energy in a sacred, grace-filled network of ninth-dimensional geometric lines. The group was helping to create the new grid of light for this universe.

You can do this too by following this visualization.

Visualization to Visit Lord Voosloo at His Retreat

1. Prepare a space where you can be relaxed and undisturbed.
2. Sit quietly and breathe comfortably with the intention of visiting Lord Voosloo's etheric retreat above Stonehenge.
3. Focus upon your activated Earth Star.
4. Ask Archangel Michael to place his deep blue cloak of protection around you.
5. Light a candle and dedicate it to being in service to Lord Voosloo's team spreading of universal sunshine and harmony.

6. Visualize yourself inside the ancient and sacred stones of Stonehenge. If you cannot imagine this, just ask to be there.
7. You are standing in the centre of a vast light-powered ascension lift. Surrounded by golden angels, it is taking you up through the dimensions into the harmonic realms of the seventh dimension.
8. Here you look at situations, people and life on Earth through a diamond angel portal. You see with angelic eyes that everything that is happening is a soul agreement. Every situation is a perfect lesson for the participants.
9. The lift takes you up to the ninth-dimensional etheric retreat of Lord Voosloo.
10. As you step out of the lift, the mighty master awaits you, glowing with joy. It is as if the gentlest but most brilliant Sun is bathing you in its light.
11. Archangel Metatron stands beside him in his golden orange shimmering radiance.
12. Together they place a ball of light into your solar plexus. This is the ninth-dimensional Instant Sun.
13. See or sense the Instant Sun expand way beyond your aura, forming a ball of ninth-dimensional light round you.
14. It is consuming all the lower energies within your four-body system.
15. Then it is contracting them until they become a small hard ball in your solar plexus.
16. And now Archangel Uriel appears and steps forwards. He pulls the small hard ball from your solar plexus and hands it to the unicorns. They take it away and transmute it.
17. As your aura expands again, Lord Voosloo fills it with his shimmering, scintillating sunshine yellow light. You may now picture your highest vision for your lifetime, which will be held in manifestation light.
18. And now ninth-dimensional energies draw in. The Gold Ray of Christ from Sirius, the blue rose from the Pleiades, the Christed Mahatma, the Cosmic Diamond Violet Flame, the White Ascension Flame, the white light of the Cosmic Heart and the love of Lady Gaia all pour into your aura.

19. Yellow-gold light streams from you and links every star, planet, galaxy and form of sacred energy in a sacred network of ninth-dimensional geometric lines. You are helping to create the new grid of light for this universe.
20. Return to where you started in the light lift and thank Lord Voosloo and Archangel Metatron.

CHAPTER 34

St Germain and Merlin

St Germain is one of the most illustrious of the ascended masters. He originated from Quishy, the ascended aspect of Saturn, and it was here that his illuminated soul took higher initiations. This enabled him to bring the spiritual discipline necessary to Earth and other training establishments in the universe. It was this path of spiritual discipline, coded into our fifth-dimensional base chakras, that enabled him to develop his powers as a magician, alchemist and immortal being. When we access our fifth-dimensional chakras we undergo similar lessons to those of St Germain in order to hone our spiritual discipline as masters.

St Germain has had an extraordinary soul journey. As an ascended master, he has had more physical incarnations than almost any other master and he has achieved immortality. At 29 years of age in each of his incarnations he undertook unusually challenging initiations to prove his worth as a leader of Saturn.

As the Comte de St Germain, a European nobleman, he was an alchemist and magician who lived for 300 years, working behind the scenes to help the world.

As Merlin in King Arthur's court, he was honoured as a sage and a wizard of natural order. He had command of the elements and worked with them every day. Whenever it was necessary to protect the secrets of Avalon, he would raise mists and make it disappear so that no one could find it. He also had command of the waters and would raise the levels of the lakes and estuaries whenever needed. Later on in that incarnation, he made his home in Tintagel, Cornwall, UK, and connected his energies to the gods of the seas. Here he worked on advanced alchemy, sending Christ Light into the waters of the planet and into the Michael ley lines surrounding the area.

He also went to Wales, where he blessed the stones for Stonehenge, filling them with magical vibrations so that they could support that two-way inter-dimensional portal. His command of alchemy enabled him to reduce the weight of the stones so that they could easily be carried to the site of Stonehenge. Then, in a druidic ceremony under the full Moon, Stonehenge was constructed to harness the vibrations of the cosmos into a seventh-dimensional portal.

St Germain incarnated several times as a Druid and pagan to uphold the natural laws. He stayed in Cornwall or on the south coast of the UK, making sure the energy of the ley lines was preserved.

As a Druid 2,000 years ago, he was very important. It was his energy that allowed the light that Jesus, Thoth and Joseph of Arimathea created on their visit to Glastonbury, UK, to flow back into the ley lines. St Germain did this with a powerful ceremony that called upon the power of the entire elemental kingdom.

In an earlier incarnation as Joseph of Egypt, he undertook incredible hardships and transcended his feelings. His ability to bi-locate enabled his soul to travel freely while his physical body was imprisoned. It was his psychic abilities that freed him to become an immensely powerful and wise counsellor to the Pharaoh.

He also had an incarnation as Samuel the prophet and founded the Rosicrucians, an order of the White Brotherhood.

In addition, St Germain has worked assiduously on the inner planes to help us. When he has been in a physical body, his spirit body has been serving on the Intergalactic Council. He often liaises with us when we have an issue to present to the council. He has continuous access to spiritual developments on Earth and is working closely with our ascension process.

For many years he was the master of the Seventh Ray, the Violet Ray of ceremonial order, magic and ritual. He brought the dispensation of the Violet Flame of Transmutation to humanity and works closely with Archangel Zadkiel, the archangel of the Violet Ray.

He is now serving as Lord of Civilization, one of the highest offices in this universe.

He is also one of the nine masters of Saturn, a group of souls in charge of the planet Saturn, who are anchoring the energy of spiritual discipline in this universe. Spiritual discipline is the foundation for bliss. When you work with St Germain, he helps you to anchor your fifth-dimensional base chakra into Saturn to access higher mastery, total faith and bliss.

Spiritual discipline was developed by the High Priests and Priestesses of Atlantis, who knew it was a foundation for enlightenment and illuminated mastery. It enabled them to master all facets of mind–body control, and yogis practise some forms of this discipline to this day.

St Germain's etheric retreat is at Mount Shasta, in northern California, USA, and you can more easily access his awesome violet light in this beautiful location.

Visualization to Work with St Germain for the Higher Good of Earth

1. Prepare for meditation. Light a candle if you choose and dedicate it to St Germain.
2. Call him to join you and bathe you in the Violet Flame.
3. Relax as the Violet Flame transmutes your four-body system and leaves you glowing and fifth-dimensional. St Germain's presence is gentle but powerful. Sense the spiritual discipline emanating from him.
4. He asks you to accompany him to his retreat in Mount Shasta. This is a seventh-dimensional retreat held in the etheric above the mountain and filled with pure violet light.
5. As you enter this energy, visualize your ascension chakras becoming completely purified.
6. St Germain asks you if there is any aspect of your personal ascension process with which you need help. You tell him about your journey and he listens to you.
7. When you have finished speaking, he tells you that you now have the opportunity to accelerate your ascension path. He invites you to attend the Halls of Spiritual Discipline in Saturn with him in your sleep.
8. Thank him for this amazing opportunity to be taught by a master of Saturn. From this point you will train with him to embrace your spiritual pathway. This is a great honour and will enable you to move forwards very rapidly.
9. St Germain now invites you to send the Violet Flame anywhere in the world that you wish to bless.
10. See waves of violet light leaving Mount Shasta and flooding Earth with grace and transmutation. Visualize everyone living in the fifth dimension and blessing Earth with their highest light.
11. Thank St Germain and return to your sacred space.
12. Open your eyes and know that you are training to be a master of Saturn, filled with faith and bliss.

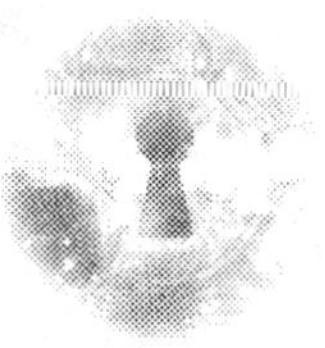

CHAPTER 35

Jesus, Bringer of Cosmic Love

After the fall of Atlantis, humans explored free will and lost contact with their souls and their true missions. The Intergalactic Council invited a great master to return to Earth for his most challenging mission yet: to bring cosmic love back to the planet to raise the frequency of all.

The great initiate chosen for this awesome mission was prepared during many incarnations for the huge challenge. He originated from Venus with no karma to resolve. He had already had incarnations as Adam, Enoch, Jeshua, Joshua and Elijah. He had also incarnated as Apollonius of Tyana, a great master teaching divine laws. In those lives only a part of his soul energy came to Earth. For his life as Jesus, however, he brought in his entire soul energy.

The Intergalactic Council and Great White Brotherhood made very careful preparations for his incarnation. Mary, the mother chosen for him, was so pure that she wasn't even allowed to touch the ground until she was four years old. She was either carried or had to stand on a shining white cloth laid out for her. This was to symbolize her purity. Her entire life was spent in preparation for the great spiritual task of giving birth to Jesus and bringing him up. She and Joseph, Jesus' father, were both Essenes. They spent several hours each day in spiritual practices and esoteric techniques, which gave them great powers and access to the sacred mysteries of the universe, including virgin birth.

Before Jesus was born, highly skilled astrologers pinpointed the position of his birth through astrological calculations. This allowed the wise men, who were El Morya, Dwjhal Khul and Lord Kuthumi, to find him. Note how Jesus was greeted and supported by Illumined Beings. Look at the people in your life and wonder who they really are!

He was born in April, as symbolized by spring lambs on Christmas cards. It wasn't until the fifth century, after years of discussion, that the Holy Fathers decreed that his official birthday should be 25 December. This is an annual date of mystic significance. Christ Light and Source love start to filter into the planet at the winter solstice, 21 December. At midnight on 24 December a cosmic change occurs, accelerating the inrush of the divine light, which then bathes us all on 25 December. Because of this, that date was celebrated as a religious festival in the ancient civilizations of India, China, Egypt and Mexico, among others. Isis, Osiris and Horus were all said to be born then, as were Bacchus, Adonis, Hercules and many of the great masters.

Just as his parents' lives were devoted to preparation for his birth, so Jesus' life was dedicated to preparing himself for his mission. His education was rigorous and carefully planned, as were his travels when he became old enough.

For three years he succeeded gloriously in carrying the Christ Light of unconditional love. When he was ready to take in the energy of the cosmic Christ, Lord Maitreya worked through him and he became a High Priest in the Order of Melchizedek.

The most beloved of the Illumined Ones, he is known as Sananda on the inner planes. This is the vibration of his Higher Self. Lady Nada is his twin flame.

Jesus' mission was to raise the light levels on Earth once again to allow the higher potential of the souls there to shine through. His incarnation was incredibly challenging, but he achieved his goal.

Upon his death in Egypt some years later, his teachings and open heart were recorded in history. He opened and anchored a vast portal to the Cosmic Heart that once again allowed light to flood our planet. For the last 2,000 years this has increased in intensity in preparation for our ascension process.

As Jesus worked with the souls of Earth, teaching the love and humility of an open heart, millions of angels flooded onto the planet and started their work. The entire plan was to pave the way for a fifth-dimensional planet and a new Golden Age.

When he was in his early forties Jesus travelled to the heart centre of the planet, which is now known as Glastonbury. He left Egypt with his wife, Mary Magdalene, and the ascended master Thoth, and met Merlin on the shores of England. These companions travelled to Avalon, where they combined their light with that of Joseph of Arimathea and carried out a task that changed the course of our energetic history.

Surrounding the heart centre of the Earth are intricate energy pathways of pure golden light known as dragon lines or ley lines. These exist all over the planet and can be described as the nerve pathways of Gaia. The original ley system was established by Thoth himself at the start of his physical life in Atlantis. As humanity became lost after the fall, the ley lines dimmed and became broken. Jesus was sent to assist with their repair.

By the time he reached Avalon, winter had gripped England. The weather was atrocious. Leaving Mary in the town of Glastonbury, Jesus, Thoth and Merlin struggled to the summit of the Tor in a howling snowstorm. On several occasions the gale-force wind sent them rolling down the steep slopes.

At the summit of the Tor was a pile of rocks. Jesus, Thoth and Merlin rearranged them into sacred geometric patterns with specially blessed crystals. They then meditated and flooded their combined energies into the heart chakra of the planet to start the repair of the sacred geometry of the land.

Thoth called forth the dragons of the Earth and asked them to carry the Christ Light round the planet. The dragons did so.

Merlin called to Master Pan, the ninth-dimensional master of nature, and to Dom, Thor and Poseidon, the masters of air, fire and water respectively, asking them to illuminate the connection of Glastonbury Tor to Venus and spread the love through the elementals.

Later, in a ceremony at the White Spring at the foot of the Tor, Jesus and Mary Magdalene used their love and divine union to anchor the divine masculine and divine feminine light into this vision.

Joseph of Arimathea then travelled to the surrounding areas and used his sacred knowledge to link the Christ Light to other sites.

All this prepared the way for the fifth-dimensional light to return some 2,000 years later – now.

When the Harmonic Convergence took place in 1987, the planet was ready to receive this light, thanks to the groundwork of these vigilant souls, who parted company and returned to their everyday lives after this trip.

Jesus' work continues on the inner planes. He is now Lord of Karma for the Eighth Ray and has recently taken on the role of Bringer of Cosmic Love, spreading love everywhere on Earth.

As pulses of light leave the Great Central Sun and the Cosmic Heart, they are received directly at Glastonbury and distributed around the planet. Just as the human heart centre is the first to wake up, so is the planetary heart. A great many souls who have been working within the current ascension process have poured their love and intention into this area to continue the work of the masters.

The web of light around the Earth now glows brightly once again. As the frequency of our planet rises sharply, the souls who live here strive to keep up with her. The dragons continue to work constantly with the elementals to help the higher energies flood to areas of need. As more hearts awaken, the light anchors and grows stronger. With the awakening of the fifth-dimensional chakra system, many masters of Earth are now remembering who they were and what their wonderful skills are.

Many are now contributing to raising the frequency of the planet and this number is increasing daily.

Visualization to Light Up the Earth

You will need a crystal for this exercise.

1. Prepare for meditation.
2. Choose a sacred spot either in your home or outside in the open air.
3. Hold your crystal in your right hand and ask for it to connect with the Cosmic Heart.
4. Feel the ninth-dimensional light of ascended Venus filling your crystal.
5. Allow this light to spread from your crystal up your arm and into your entire body.
6. See and feel your chakras glowing.

7. When your crystal is full of golden light, place it between your feet and connect it to your Earth Star chakra.
8. See your Earth Star starting to glow bright liquid silver.
9. Visualize the light from your crystal merging with your Earth Star and travelling into the planet.
10. See this mixture of golden-silver light flowing into the ley lines surrounding where you are sitting. Wherever you are will be lit up very brightly.
11. Call upon the mighty earth dragons to carry this light to wherever it is most needed. You may even have somewhere specific in mind.
12. As your light travels around the world, see it glowing more intensely.
13. Ask Archangels Sandalphon and Metatron to anchor the higher aspects of Heaven into Earth and sit quietly while they perform this planetary task. When you feel that the light has been anchored, thank them.
14. Thank the earth dragons also and take a few deep breaths.
15. When you are ready, open your eyes and know that you have performed powerful planetary work.

CHAPTER 36

The Goddess Masters

This chapter is for men as well as women. It is for all those who will benefit from developing their qualities of feminine mastery.

For the past 10,000 years, since the decline of Atlantis, there has been a collective unconscious belief that men are powerful and superior to women. Those who have incarnated in female bodies have had to push beyond this belief to accomplish mastery. This still applies nowadays, but not in such an extreme way as before.

It is never easy to move the barriers of the collective unconscious and yet everyone's perspectives and expectations have shifted dramatically in recent years. Who thought people would fly in aeroplanes? Or carry their phones around with them? Or be able to receive information anywhere on mini portable computers? Or run around on artificial legs? The technological age has expanded the boundaries of our beliefs. And as we see things from an expanded perspective, we are becoming more enlightened.

The advent of spiritual technology will wake people up even more quickly. And because spiritual technology is dependent on the right-brain conception of new ideas and visions, women will come to the fore.

Many of the great masters, especially women, have tried valiantly to hold their light and integrity in the face of the consciousness of humanity. This has pushed them into very challenging initiations through which change has been instigated on the planet. Their courage and dedication have led to the development of qualities that have greatly illuminated their auras. The light that they have earned helps all those who aspire to become walking masters.

Mary/Isis

The great initiate Mary gave virgin birth to Jesus in one incarnation and, as Isis, gave virgin birth to Horus in another. This was a moral dilemma, as the concept of virgin birth was not understood then. It is still incomprehensible until you vibrate at the illumined upper levels of the fifth dimension. Then you know that every single conception is part physical and part spiritual. In certain cases, where the female participant is very pure and high frequency, the spiritual transcends the limitations of the physical act. However, when Mary and Isis at a soul level agreed to the conception of Jesus and Horus, their surrender to the will of God enabled doors to massive world transformation to open.

If their story touches you, tune into their energy. By doing so you will access the qualities that enabled them to stand in their mastery.

Joan of Arc/Madame Blavatsky/Catherine of Siena

As a great visionary, Joan of Arc had extraordinary conviction and passion. Though she was simply a peasant girl in medieval France, both St Michael and St Catherine appeared to her, impressing on her that she was the saviour of the country and that God wished her to lead the French army to victory over the English. She was told she must speak to Charles, the Dauphin, and in order to journey to see him she had to cut her hair and dress as a man. She did lead the French army and won a great battle at Orléans. However, her final initiation during that lifetime was to be burned at the stake. This purified her and enabled her to ascend spectacularly.

Her second incarnation was as the 19th-century Russian woman Helena Blavatsky, who channelled Dwjhal Khul and founded the Theosophical Society. Surmounting her challenges, she succeeded in establishing one of the White Flames in the world.

In another life, in 14th-century Italy, she was Catherine of Siena. In this life, she had mystic and religious visions from childhood. When she grew up, she led a very strict and pure life and founded an extremely strict religious order. She tried to be a peace ambassador and wrote many letters to promote amity. She died at the age of 33. This is the number of the Christ Light. She is now working on the inner planes to bring spirituality into religion.

Great visionaries still lead very challenging lives. Even now psychics and people with spiritual ideas are ahead of their time, but can be helped by accessing the energies of Joan of Arc/Madame Blavatsky/Catherine of Siena. If you wish to be one of those who carry the White Ascension Flame to bring peace and light to humanity, tune into this mighty being.

Quan Yin

Quan Yin is known as the Goddess of Mercy thanks to the love, compassion and wisdom she demonstrated during her 2,000-year incarnation in China. During this long period of time she chose to stay on Earth in a physical body to assist humanity, though she learned to be multi-dimensional. She lived in the seventh dimension, but could lower her frequency to the fifth dimension, where she could maintain her physical body, and also raise it to the ninth dimension. She required no food, but when in the fifth dimension she enjoyed fruit and vegetables, the lighter delights of Earth. As lightworkers become walking masters, more of us are becoming multi-dimensional, too, and we can call on Quan Yin to help us.

Her dragon friends helped her, travelling like a protective army with her through the frequency bands and enabling her to flow over and through challenges. Her great love was for the Eastern world, where dragons were understood and considered to be part of life. Dragons are now pouring back into the world, East and West, and Quan Yin is helping people to open their consciousness to accept them and work with them. As a master, she now embraces the entire planet and bathes us all in her love.

She has long been regarded as the Eastern equivalent of Mother Mary and all her current service for Earth is about bringing the divine feminine into the consciousness of humanity. Currently she serves on the Intergalactic Council, where her role is to spread the divine feminine wisdom. She is particularly concerned with empowering women and her influence can be felt in many women's organizations. She is also opening the minds of teachers everywhere, as well as those working in prisons and even in government and business.

Whatever the situation, she sends in light to help men become more in touch with their feminine side. She is responsible for the spread of male bonding groups and for men becoming more interested in the raising of small children and all activities that help them embrace their wiser, softer side.

As the master of the Sixth Ray on the Board of the Lords of Karma, she is also helping to bring balance into religion and spirituality.

Tune into the great goddess master Quan Yin if you wish to spread her light on Earth.

If you feel your mission is to expand the enlightenment of the world in some way by extending the collective understanding of the qualities of men and women, you may like to connect with the goddess masters in this section.

Visualization to Connect with Mother Mary and Quan Yin

1. Find a place where you can be quiet and undisturbed.
2. Visualize yourself in a power spot, where the energy of the Earth and the beauty of the place strengthens you. Take your time to absorb this energy.
3. It is most important to relax, so breathe in the peace and beauty around you until you feel calm and centred.
4. Think about your mission or what you would like to accomplish next with the help of the great goddess masters. All things are becoming possible.
5. Invite them to come to you to assist you.
6. Be aware of Mother Mary or Isis standing in front of you. Her energy body like a vast scintillating ball of aquamarine and gold light. The light she has earned is radiating from her.
7. Step forwards so that you are standing inside her pulsing ball of high-frequency light and power.
8. Feel her energy working on you, healing you, strengthening you, bringing you wisdom, empowering you and lighting you up with her higher qualities. Take your time and keep breathing.
9. As she withdraws, thank her.
10. And now be aware of Joan of Arc and/or Madame Blavatsky and/or Catherine of Siena (it may be one or all of them) standing in front of you

in their huge energy body of shimmering and flowing blue, green and gold light.

11. Step forwards so that you are standing inside their pulsing ball of high-frequency light and power.
12. Feel their energy working on you, healing you, strengthening you, bringing you wisdom, empowering you and lighting you up with their higher qualities. Take your time and keep breathing.
13. As they withdraw, thank them.
14. And now be aware of the Goddess of Mercy and Compassion, Quan Yin, standing in front of you in her huge, radiant and flowing energy body of magenta, white, gold and diamond light.
15. Feel her energy working on you, healing you, strengthening you, bringing you wisdom, empowering you and lighting you up with her higher qualities. Take your time and keep breathing.
16. As she withdraws, thank her.
17. An extraordinary transformation has taken place in your own energy fields. You can do anything you need to for the highest good.

CHAPTER 37

Influence of the Goddess Masters

Several of the great goddess masters have dedicated themselves to bringing in a new understanding of spiritual perspectives to us on Earth and are currently working on the inner planes to impress spirituality rather than religion into the minds of humanity. Here are some of those who made a big difference during their lifetimes and are continuing to do so with their work in spirit. The roles and responsibilities of walking masters in physical bodies can be awesome. And we are rarely aware of it.

Also, please remember that you may also be doing this work while incarnated. You may even be an aspect of one of these magnificent masters, carrying some of their energy in your aura. You may be a great master yourself and be surprised at the power of your light, which you will only know when you see who you truly are. This happens when you reach higher enlightenment or after death.

Mary Magdalene

Mary Magdalene was an Essene and a highly evolved master in her lifetime. She incarnated with Jesus and became his spiritual partner. Together they walked the chakra trail with their daughter, Sarah. Mary Magdalene's reputation was vilified during her lifetime and people have continued to judge her.

She has been training on the inner planes for many years to bring healing and spirituality into the light of Sixth Ray, the ray of idealism and devotion, taking over from Jesus as its master.

In addition she serves on the Intergalactic Council and her task is to oversee the lighting up of religions with spirituality. She holds the vision of unified love for the world.

If you want to develop transcendent love, tune into Mary Magdalene.

St Clare

In her physical lifetime, Clare was born into a rich Italian family and enjoyed a privileged childhood. However, she yearned for a life of piety and simplicity. She was very inspired by St Francis of Assissi (an incarnation of Lord Kuthumi), and consequently left her comfortable family life to become a nun. Eventually she founded the Order of Poor Clares. These nuns took vows of poverty and dedicated themselves to serving those in need.

In the spirit realms St Clare is working to bring greater spiritual awareness to humanity. She is one of a team of three female masters who are co-operating to raise the frequency of humanity. The other two are Catherine of Siena and St Teresa d'Ávila.

When the time is appropriate, St Clare will incarnate again and during that lifetime at a soul level she will report back to Lord Kuthumi, the World Teacher, on the progress there has been in raising spiritual awareness on Earth. She will also relate to him what needs to be done to help this process.

If you hold a vision that requires grit and determination, tune into St Clare.

St Teresa d'Ávila

St Teresa has experienced many incarnations, most of them as a religious mystic and visionary. In her lifetime as St Teresa, in Spain in the 16th century, her mother died when she was very young and she was brought up by nuns. She eventually reformed the Carmelite order, overcoming much opposition in her quest.

During her lifetimes she gathered a team of lightworkers round her and many of them work with her now on the inner planes. Huge numbers of others have joined them.

The walking masters on Earth are training for their greater roles in the spirit world, where they take on much responsibility and have a profound influence. St Teresa is currently endeavouring to bring through religion without dogma, based on spirituality and Oneness with All That Is.

If you wish to hold the Flame of Oneness, tune into St Teresa d'Ávila.

Lady Nada

Lady Nada is so called because she has no ego. *Nada* literally means 'nothing'. She is the twin flame of Sananda, the Higher Self of Jesus.

During one incarnation she was Elizabeth, the mother of John the Baptist. She was also alive at the time of the prophet Mohammed and promoted Islamic art.

She is currently the master of the Seventh Ray, the ray of ritual, ceremony and magic. This ray will predominate in the new Golden Age of Aquarius and will enable the spiritual and physical to blend. She still sits, however, on the board of the Lords of Karma in charge of the Third Ray.

Until recently she also served on the Intergalactic Council, but her promotion has meant that she is now spreading cosmic love to the universe.

She is helping people to remember ancient healing methods and wisdom and is bringing forwards the 'alternative' and 'natural' methods that are gaining influence now. She is also teaching those who will use their gifts for the highest good to become more psychic and to listen to their intuition.

If you are ready to promote ancient healing methods and wisdom as well as spread cosmic love, tune into Lady Nada.

Pallas Athena

Pallas Athena was a chief counsellor in Lemuria and then a High Priestess in Atlantis working in the Temple of Truth.

She represents the Fourth Ray of harmony through conflict on the Karmic Board. She carries the quality of integrity for all on Earth and helps all those who are bringing truth forwards.

If you wish to develop truth and integrity and spread harmony, tune into Pallas Athena.

Lady Portia

Lady Portia is known as the Goddess of Liberty. She was a High Priestess in the Temple of Liberty in Atlantis. She works a little with individuals to help them to be mentally and emotionally free. Mostly, however, she holds the Flame of Freedom with Paul the Venetian to enable humanity to walk the ascension path. It is time for us to be free to experience Earth as it was intended we should.

Lady Portia's task is to bring back the energy of Golden Atlantis. She is the spokesperson for the Seventh Ray on the Karmic Board.

If you wish to be one of those who holds the Flame of Freedom on Earth and accelerate the return of the energy of Golden Atlantis, tune into Lady Portia.

Visualization to Connect with More Goddess Masters

1. Find a place where you can be quiet and undisturbed. Light a candle if you can.
2. Take a moment to relax and centre yourself so you are ready to absorb the energy of the goddess masters.
3. Visualize yourself walking along a golden path, lit with jewels, towards a golden temple in the sky.
4. Golden dragons are circling the temple, holding the frequency high. Fire dragons protect the entrance. They nod a welcome to you.
5. As you enter through a vast shimmering golden gate, you smell a beautiful fragrance and hear angelic music.
6. You walk into a sunny walled courtyard, cascading with flowers.
7. The goddess masters Mary Magdalene, St Clare, St Teresa d'Ávila, Lady Nada, Pallas Athena and Lady Portia await you with open hearts radiating love and light.
8. Tell them all that you wish to develop goddess master qualities or, if you want to address one master in particular, do so.
9. As one, they rise and surround you, linking hands.
10. You find yourself in the centre of a huge circle of swirling gold and rainbow light.
11. You may feel energies within you being unlocked, codes being lit up and rusty old beliefs you no longer need being removed.
12. Each goddess master places a flame in your aura:

    Mary Magdalene places a deep pink one.
    St Clare a pale blue one.
    St Teresa d'Ávila a deep blue one
    Lady Nada a pale pink one
    Pallas Athena a golden one.
    Lady Portia a shimmering white one.

13. As the goddess masters step back, feel their brilliant lights drawing away from you.
14. Know that you have received a divine feminine light bath and give thanks.
15. Return through the golden gate and down the path to where you started.
16. Sense that you have stepped into new possibilities of mastery and enlightenment.

The Dragon Kingdom

CHAPTER 38

Dragons

Dragons are elementals – beings who do not contain all four elements of earth, air, fire and water – and they are of the angelic realms, at a frequency beyond our limited visual capacity.

They have worked with the planet since Earth began. During the birth of the planet, a time known as the first Golden Age of Angala, they helped to change Earth from a ball of fire into a living, breathing world. They worked with Archangel Metatron and the creative force of Shekinah to build the original continental forms on Earth. They also helped to establish the ley lines, which is why they were originally called dragon lines.

A Golden Age is so called because the people and the land radiate a blazing golden aura. There have been five of these very high-frequency times so far.

The first was Angala, the birth of the planet, to which the dragon kingdom contributed their special powers. It was an eternal moment, so its vital creative force can be accessed at any time.

The second was the Golden Age of Africa, known as the Age of Petranium. Very high-frequency beings from throughout the universes answered the clarion call to be part of this experience, which took place in Africa and to a lesser extent in Asia. This was a time when Africa was rich, verdant and abundant, and the energy remains within the land, to return when the people are ready. Dragons helped to establish this era both in Africa and Asia, working with the seventh-dimensional beings who lived there in etheric bodies.

During this time only seventh-dimensional dragons were on Earth. These dragons have the power to create or destroy matter. So earth and fire dragons helped to carve out mountains, while water dragons purified the water and illuminated it with the Christ consciousness. Wherever they swam, golden light spread out through the water. Air dragons helped to keep everything moving.

Later the dragons handed the maintenance of this extraordinary and high-frequency age to the angelic forces and the seventh-dimensional etheric walking masters of Africa.

The third Golden Age of Mu was based in the Pacific and preceded Lemuria. This was the time of the dinosaurs. The Earth was also inhabited by fourth to fifth-dimensional etheric beings who left no trace of their presence, but they did very much love and assist nature. They still hold the healing blue aquamarine flame of Michael and Mary within Hollow Earth and the hollow centres of Neptune, Orion, Sirius and the Pleiades.

The dragons co-operated with the beings of Mu to spread the light of the Flame of Michael and Mary through the ley lines of Earth and into the auras of the ascension planets, stars and galaxies. As a result of their service work, at the end of this civilization these particular dragons ascended into the fifth dimension.

The fourth Golden Age of Lemuria was also based in the Pacific and took place at a time when humans were non-physical fifth-dimensional beings. The Lemurians were a fifth-dimensional light force, rather like angels, but vibrating at a lower frequency. They loved Earth and passionately wanted to help it. Even then it was known that it would be going through a critical phase in the very distant future between 2012 and 2032!

The Lemurians left an awesome gift specifically to help us with the amazing transition we are undergoing right now. They took light from Source and merged it with special qualities from the auras of the stars, planets and great energies of the universe, focused it until it formed a molten mass and then poured it into the dragon lines, where it formed high-frequency Lemurian crystals. This enabled the planet to radiate light from within.

Dragons have been protecting these special seams of Lemurian light to help us through this transition period and into the next Golden Age. The word 'dragon' originally meant 'watcher' or 'guardian'. Dragons have also been looking after all that the Lemurians loved – the land, nature and the people of Earth. They really are our great companions, defenders, protectors and carers.

At the end of the time of Lemuria, the etheric beings prayed that they might be allowed to take physical bodies and experience life in an entirely new form. They wished to experience the senses and also to represent the energies of Archangels Metatron and Shekinah in a physical form in order to ground their light into the planet.

Their request was granted on the understanding that the participants in this experiment also had emotions. A clarion call went out and, as with previous great opportunities, souls volunteered from all over the universes. No one had experienced physicality before and the dragons assisted these new humans. They first assisted the Lemurians in building structures on Earth to prepare for the experiment and then they cleared the energy round the first Atlanteans so that everything flowed easily for them.

Dragons helped to carve the mountain of Poseida on which stood the great Temple of Atlantis, known as the Temple of Poseidon, which housed the Great Crystal of Atlantis. They also protected this crystalline power generator. When it fell into the centre of the Bermuda Triangle at the end of Atlantis, water dragons took on the responsibility of protecting it, for it was still an active inter-dimensional portal and great power generator.

When the Intergalactic Council needed to use the portal, the light created was so intense that everything and everyone within the triangle went through an inter-dimensional shift. This meant that to our human eyes they disappeared. Of course their souls agreed to this and it provided an opportunity for spiritual promotion.

In the past this portal was frequently needed and so the mystery of the Bermuda Triangle was born. Now, because the planet has risen in frequency, when the inter-dimensional portal is opened, it does not have such an impact on the people and matter around it.

In 2015 it was time for the Great Crystal to rise again. The dragons released the protection they had held around it so that the full force of its light rose up like a fountain to illuminate Earth once more. This has had a dramatic impact on the ascension and mastery process on the planet.

At the fall of Atlantis, all those thousands of years ago, the dragons made a huge sacrifice: they gave up their ascended roles and adopted fourth-dimensional etheric bodies so that they would be ready to assist us during the mighty transition we are undergoing right now. So they became a focus of stories and fairy tales. They were etched in the blueprint of everyone who had incarnated with them during the Golden Era, however, and this kept their memory alive. Those who consciously or unconsciously believed in them could draw a fourth-dimensional dragon helper to them.

At the Harmonic Convergence in 1987, at the start of the 25-year period of purification of the planet, this memory of dragons allowed many of these wise creatures to return to the planet. They reconnected at a high level.

In 2011 and 2012 there was a huge boost in dragon energy as the 33 cosmic portals started to open. The opening of the sacred portal of Lemuria allowed a vast amount of dragon light to return to the planet. The cosmic portals in Andorra and in Honolulu are also dragon portals and an influx of these wise creatures occurred from there. So many dragons entered Earth at this point that they immediately outnumbered humans two to one. And these portals will continue to open and to illuminate humanity until they are fully operational in 2032. This means huge opportunities for mastery and enlightenment are now available.

Dragons are now ushering in very high frequencies and solidifying them. They are such mighty beings that everyone on the pathway to mastery is being urged to connect with them. You, as a seeker, can do this at any time during your journey, but is becoming imperative now, as the veils between the dimensions become increasingly thinner.

In 2013, before writing *The Archangel Guide to Ascension*, Tim was directly contacted by dragons as he was walking outside and connecting with nature. A voice stated very clearly, 'We are the dragon forces and we are at your service.'

At first Tim was a bit unsettled by this, as he had not been approached by dragons before. As with any connection from an outside energy source, he decided to take the energy into his heart to verify that it was pure. It was of the utmost purity and integrity. Two days later, he started working with these mighty beings and was introduced to the vast realm of light and love that they have to offer.

Visualization to Connect to Dragons and Their Energy

1. Prepare for meditation.
2. Choose a quiet and peaceful place and light a candle. If you have crystals, place them around you in a circle.
3. Invoke the Cosmic Diamond Violet Flame and let it soak through your body and fields. Feel this violet light alchemizing every molecule of your being into light.
4. As you transform into higher light, bring your attention to your third eye centre. Go deep into it.
5. You are moving back through time and space to a point where there was complete darkness.
6. See a bright light in front of you and move towards it. The closer you get to it, the brighter it becomes.
7. It is a molten mass of moving fire. You realize that you are witnessing the birth of a world in the early days of the universe. It is Earth.
8. Around this ball of fire, you see two vast Universal Angels, Metatron and Shekinah. They are gently tending to the ball, shaping it with love and kindness.
9. They pause, and from their glowing golden hearts thousands of dragons pour out, representing the elements, energies and light rays that will form and will construct the brand new world.
10. See these newborn dragons go to work immediately, all with different roles and tasks to perform. Earth dragons are creating solid land. Water dragons are creating the molecular structures of the seas. Fire dragons are carving golden geometric lines around the globe, establishing the blueprint for the ley lines. Air dragons are breathing forth the first winds.
11. You realize that you are witnessing a greatly speeded up construction process.

12. A beautiful golden dragon approaches you. He introduces himself as the Christed Master Dragon, keeper of the Christ consciousness for all beings who dwell on Earth.
13. As you connect to this mighty being, you feel every one of your ascension chakras light up:

    The golden dragon blesses your Stellar Gateway chakra, lighting it up so that it shines bright gold.

    He blesses your soul star chakra, opening the magenta and blue doorway to all your spiritual gifts and talents.

    He blesses your causal chakra, connecting you fully to the highest archangel and unicorn light possible.

    He blesses your crown, releasing liquid golden codes of inner wisdom from your soul.

    He blesses your third eye, allowing you to see through your veils of illusion and deep into your true mastery.

    He blesses your throat, completely releasing any past-life agreements that have prevented you from speaking your master truth.

    He blesses your heart, lighting it up with the purest Christ Light and expanding the chakra so that it runs from shoulder to shoulder.

    He blesses your solar plexus, completely releasing any energies that do not belong to you.

    He blesses your navel, merging you with all beings in all dimensions throughout the multi-verse.

    He blesses your sacral, illuminating you with the deepest transcendent love.

    He blesses your base, anchoring in the full power of your mighty I Am Presence.

    And finally, he blesses your Earth Star, connecting you fully with all of the wisdom of the many Golden Ages that have prepared Earth for this ascension process.

14. Take a few moments to integrate this light fully. You have just received a blessing only bestowed upon masters who have passed many challenges.
15. The golden dragon invites you to sit upon his back and flies you back to your current reality.
16. Thank this beautiful being for his amazing gift and open your eyes.
17. Ask Archangels Metatron and Sandalphon to ground you into the Great Central Sun and deep into Hollow Earth.
18. Ask the fire dragons to surround your ascension pathway with the brightest fire.
19. Know you are one step closer to walking mastery.

CHAPTER 39

Working with Dragons

When a soul on the ascension path starts to wake up, a fourth-dimensional elemental dragon that reflects their birth sign will come to work with them. So these dragons will be earth, air, fire or water dragons, and occasionally a mixture. If, however, your mission requires the talents of a specific elemental dragon, that one will step forwards. For example, if your soul journey means that you are using your psychic abilities or navigating the worlds of dreams and imagination or spending much time in or on physical water, you may attract a water dragon.

Diana is a Virgo, which is an earth sign, and she has a fire dragon because she needs one to burn up any energies that prevent her work from moving forwards. Like many people, she also helps to hold visions for the fifth-dimensional communities and the golden cities of the next era as well as the new way of being in the imminent Age of Aquarius, so she also needs a fire dragon to assist with the formation of this future on the planet.

Tim is a fire sign, so he automatically has a fire dragon.

Your dragon is your greatest companion, protection and support. Your guardian angel also performs these tasks, but angels work on different frequency bands from dragons. Dragons can physically clear lower energies around you and manipulate matter for your highest good. Angels hold the blueprint for your highest potential and drop your best course of action into your consciousness.

Many people unconsciously believe in the spiritual realms, though they might deny it in the waking world. Diana's mother was an avid disbeliever, though she was very tuned into nature, which automatically opens people up to divine energies. Diana spent her early childhood in the Himalayas. Though the family moved frequently when she was a child, one permanent fixture was a tall wooden dragon used as a standard lamp. He was called Duggie and stood in the hall. He even returned to the UK with the family.

When Diana moved into an understanding of and communication with the spiritual realms, she met her dragon. At first she thought he was called Duggie, but he laughed (a dragon laugh) and said that Duggie was the name of her mother's dragon, who obviously connected unconsciously to him! Diana's dragon is called Douglas. From their name vibrations she knew the dragons were very connected.

How Can Dragons Help You?

Protection

Diana is not very keen on driving, but she had to motor across the continent to the south of France with her dog, Venus. Every time she got into the car she asked Douglas and the dragons to clear the way in front of her, angels to surround the car and unicorns to light the way above it. The whole way she felt as if she was in a total cocoon of safety and did not have a moment's concern.

Nightmares

Nightmares are usually the result of emotions held in your unconscious mind from this life or a previous one that are calling to be set free. When you sleep, the gateway between your unconscious and your conscious mind opens and the memories surface. The emotions attached to the memories are held in your emotional body and on the collective astral plane. As you sleep, your spirit travels through the astral planes to the spiritual ones. If it meets an emotion, that emotion will surface for your attention. Sensitive people and children in particular are impacted by this.

If you ask your dragon, it will clear the way for you when you travel during your sleep. It will also consume any energy it needs to so that you can enjoy pure sleep.

You can ask your child's dragon to guard them too. It often helps to give your child a toy dragon or a little model one that can sit protectively by their bedside.

Cleansing the Planet

If you watch television or hear the news, you will be aware that there are pockets of energy that need to be cleansed. Some of these go deep into the land itself. You can send in fire dragons to consume all that is not love. Then ask unicorns to fly above the land and hold the light in that place. You can do massive and wonderful service work by asking fire dragons and angelic forces to cleanse places.

Cleansing Our Waters

Water dragons can purify the beautiful waters of our planet. If you have a water dragon, you can be particularly effective by asking them to go to places that need to be cleansed. Our waters are calling out to return to their pristine pure, love-filled natural state, so that around 2010 Archangel Metatron sent an invitation into the universe for beings to help bring this about. Elementals called kyhils responded and in exchange for spiritual promotion they are bringing our beautiful oceans back to purity again.

Christed Golden Dragons

These wonderful golden fifth-dimensional dragons are bringing pure love to the planet. If asked, they will surround ceremonies or special occasions like weddings or birthday parties and protect them.

Pink Dragons of Love

Under the direction of the great master Quan Yin, pink dragons bearing the glorious light of transcendent love poured onto the planet at the Cosmic Moment when the portal of Honolulu started to open.

These luminous pink dragons go to individuals and families and dissolve anything that prevents them from experiencing love or fulfilling their potential. Like bright pink lights, they illuminate situations so that everyone involved sees from a higher perspective with the eyes of love. The dragons melt away old sexual beliefs so that healing and happiness return. Call on them and they will come to you.

Quan Yin is often seen by sensitives travelling with a pink dragon wrapped around her shoulders.

Violet Dragons

When it is time to transmute energies in a place, situation or around people, you can call in violet dragons. These wondrous dragons work with the Violet Flame or independently and can set you free. When you are fifth-dimensional, they are ready and waiting for you to direct them.

As we move into the new Golden Age, a few people will still be at the upper levels of the fourth dimension and some of the dragons will remain in their fourth-dimensional bodies to assist them. They will perform a final cleansing so that the planet can shine again.

The majority of humans will be fifth-dimensional, so fifth-dimensional dragons will help them create the new Golden Age. They will be stabilizing the higher energy and putting violet fire in where it is necessary as the transition takes place.

Black Dragons

Black has always been the colour of the divine feminine, indicating the dark cave where secret treasures and wisdom are kept safe. And black dragons are very protective, wise and mysterious. They help those on the path to enlightenment and mastery to connect with their own deepest wisdom. When black dragons connect with you, know that you are on the right path.

Dragon Mastery

Throughout history certain people have had a great affinity with dragons and learned to guide and control them with the power of their minds and hearts: they have become dragon masters.

Master Abraham was one of the best-known dragon masters. He was an aspect of El Morya, who was a High Priest in Atlantis and a priest in the Order of Melchizidek. You can invoke Master Abraham if you want to train or serve as a dragon master on the inner planes. This also involves helping others to understand the powers of the dragons and the true extent to their service work.

Quan Yin, as mentioned earlier, is often seen with a dragon. There are literally hundreds of images of her on the internet with fire, earth, air and water dragons. Many of them depict her travelling with a dragon in its element or controlling the element. For example, she calms huge waves or roaring winds.

As part of your journey to enlightenment and mastery, you, too, may want to become a dragon master. The journey to dragon mastery is:

- Develop the best dragon qualities, which are both masculine and feminine. Be kind, caring, companionable, fierce, strong, powerful, open and generous-hearted. Control your emotions and be a beacon of light to help others.
- Master the elements (*as described in Chapter 41*).
- Stand in your power at all times.

Visualization: A Dragon Blessing

1. Prepare for meditation.
2. Call to the fire dragons to clear and illuminate your sacred space. Feel them swirling around you clockwise and anti-clockwise, lighting up your surroundings with golden fire.
3. Ask the dragons to move through your four-body system, clearing anything from you which you feel you need to release. Feel it being dissolved with sacred flames.
4. With your eyes closed, call on a dragon representative to introduce itself to you. It can be any size, colour or energy. Allow it to sit quietly with you and feel its energy.
5. Bring your attention to your heart centre. Visualize it glowing pure, radiant white. See the heart of your dragon companion also glowing brightly in the centre of its magnificent chest.
6. Allow a beam of light to flow from your master heart chakra and join with that of the dragon. Feel the union between the two of you, the oneness.
7. Tell the dragon anything that you wish from the centre of your heart. Be

truthful, loving and honest. Dragons have infinite wisdom.

8. Wait for a response. If you have asked a question, the answer may come to you later as a sign or synchronicity.
9. Invoke Archangel Gabriel to place a radiant diamond in your dragon's heart, and thank the dragon for coming to you and also for its selfless service to humanity and the Earth.
10. Ask Gabriel and his legions of angels to bestow this blessing upon all of the dragons working upon Earth at this time. See them all with their hearts shining with diamond light.
11. Thank Archangel Gabriel and know that you have offered a great service to the working dragons of Gaia.

CHAPTER 40

How Dragons Help You Master Your Soul Mission

Your soul mission is usually whatever you love to do. It fulfils you and makes you feel that your life is worthwhile. Very often you can only see as far as the next step of your mission and you can ask the dragons to help you reach this. You can also perform a dragon ceremony to help you reach any goal, as long as it is for your highest good.

Water Dragons

Diana was walking in the forest one day thinking about her soul mission. At that time water was trying to teach her something. She had several leaks in her house that were taking time, money and effort to sort out. And now the hose from her jacuzzi had sheared off, depositing the contents of her bath through the ceiling of her room dedicated to Metatron. It seemed there was a clear spiritual message for her.

She called in the water dragons and asked them to help her learn what the water was endeavouring to bring to her attention.

Immediately she was surrounded by dozens of greeny-blue water dragons, like serpents. They were all facing in the direction that she was walking, undulating as they streamed beside her. While she was moving forwards, this was perfect: Diana felt she was in the current with them. But when she stopped and stood still, they turned and twisted round her: they no longer flowed. She realized they were telling her she must keep moving in pace with the universe.

When she understood that message, they reminded her that water was flexible and took the path of least resistance. She realized that now they were telling her to be flexible and to find ways of negotiating and flowing round obstacles and problems rather than facing them head on.

When she stroked them, it was like stroking very soft cats. Even though they didn't have fur, they felt silky and smooth. This was reminding her to call on their feminine energies. She was much more used to calling on the fire dragons, with their fiercely masculine qualities, but the presence of the water dragons offered a new insight about ways to move forwards.

Diana thanked the water dragons. Since then, they have appeared beside her whenever she has thought about them, waving and undulating through the air and reminding her of their many qualities, such as flow, flexibility, purification and cleansing, and, most important of all, that water carries the love of the universe. Always do everything with love.

Air Dragons

Playful blue air dragons help you to bring the very important qualities of lightness and fun into your soul journey. You miss the purpose when you march along your path head down like a determined bull, looking neither to the right nor the left. You miss opportunities when you are so focused on your destination that you don't see the delights of the walk. Life is not intended to be a route march.

Ask the air dragons to lighten up your life and bring fun into your days. You may be surprised what happens. And you have to be willing to participate in the enjoyment. Actively join in everything that is offered to you, or the air dragons will swirl off to play elsewhere.

When you have relaxed and enjoyed what has been presented to you, the air dragons will metaphorically fill your sails with wind so that you speed along.

Earth Dragons

The wonderful earth dragons encourage you to be grounded and solid, to put down roots and to cleanse the land you live and walk on. At the same time they love it when you dance strong, powerful, energetic dances, pounding the earth as you raise your kundalini. Earth dragons actively work with you to raise your inner serpent, for this lifts your frequency so that life can bring you great rewards. It also keeps you in touch with the Earth and Lady Gaia, who automatically connect you to your soul mission.

Fire Dragons

The powerful and energetic bright orange fire dragons are irrepressible in their efforts to consume and burn up everything that is needed to free you up. They love to clear your soul path and light up your way like flaming beacons. They fire you with enthusiasm and are the fiercest protectors. They can help you massively on your soul journey.

The many other dragons will also help you on your soul mission. The violet dragons will transmute the old, the pink dragons will bring in higher love, the golden Christed dragons will give you love, wisdom and protection. The black dragons, who work with Archangel Sandalphon, will carry the deepest and wisest secrets of the universe.

When you engage with all the dragons, they help you balance your masculine and feminine qualities, your work and play, your ability to be grounded and to fly. You master the elements of your life and really enjoy life on Earth.

A Dragon Ceremony

Here is a ceremony you can do to ask the dragons to light up your mission and help you reach your destiny.

To Prepare for a Dragon Ceremony

1. Write down clearly your mission or what you want the dragons to help you achieve.
2. You may like to create an altar on which to place items to represent the dragons of the elements:

   Find something to represent water dragons. A bowl of water is fine, or a vase of flowers.

   Air dragons can be represented by a feather, a leaf or a model of an angel, unicorn or fairy, who are all of the element of air.

   Earth dragons can be represented by a crystal or pebble, some soil or a growing plant.

   Fire dragons can be represented by a candle or by fire.

   Violet, pink, golden and black dragons can be represented by a piece of cloth or a crystal or object of the appropriate colour.

3. If you particularly want to work with certain dragons, note the following:

   If you particularly want to work with water dragons, do the ceremony by an ocean, river or lake. It is most powerful at the full Moon.

   If you particularly want to work with air dragons, do the ceremony on a hilltop or in a windy place in the morning or at a weekend.

   If you particularly want to work with earth dragons, do the ceremony outside at a sacred site or beauty spot where the earth energies are very powerful.

If you particularly want to work with fire dragons, do the ceremony by a blazing fire or a bonfire in the evening when the light can be seen.

If you particularly want to work with violet dragons, use a voilet cloth (*see Step 5, page 231*) and do the ceremony within a ring of amethyst crystals or place a large amethyst crystal in the centre of your circle.

If you particularly want to work with pink dragons, place a pink cloth (*see Step 6, page 231*) or pink quartz crystals in a heart shape on your altar.

If you particularly want to work with golden dragons, place something golden on your altar.

If you particularly want to work with black dragons, place a black cloth (*see Step 8, page 231*) black obsidian on your altar and do the ceremony after dark.

Dragons Help Your Soul Mission Ceremony

1. Place your object to represent the water dragons on the altar with the words:

   'I call on the beloved water dragons to stream with me in the shortest and easiest way to my mission and help me flow to success.'

2. Place your object to represent the air dragons on the altar with the words:

   'I call on the beloved air dragons to waft me towards my mission, to make my journey light and fun and to blow me in the direction of success.'

3. Place your object to represent the earth dragons on the altar with the words:

   'I call on the beloved earth dragons to connect me to Lady Gaia and ground and energize my journey to my mission.'

4. Place your candle on the altar and light it with the words:

   'I call on the beloved fire dragons to blaze a trail in front of and around me. Please act as beacons lighting my way towards my soul mission.'

5. Place your violet cloth or amethyst crystal(s) on the altar with the words:

   'I call on the beloved violet dragons to purify the energy round my soul mission, then to spiral me towards success.'

6. Place your pink cloth or rose quartz crystal on the altar with the words:

   'I call on the beloved pink dragons to fill my soul mission and everyone connected with it with love.'

7. Place your gold cloth or golden object on the altar with the words:

   'I call on the beloved golden dragons to fill me and my soul mission with Christ Light.'

8. Place your black cloth or obsidian crystal on the altar with the words:

   'I call on the beloved black dragons of divine feminine wisdom to fill me with deepest wisdom regarding my soul mission and to lead me to its fruition.'

9. Read aloud your soul mission.
10. You may like to dance or sing or meditate.
11. Thank the dragons.

CHAPTER 41

Mastery of the Elements and Nature

The occurrence of a breeze, hurricane, earthquake, storm, flood or major fire is dependent on a number of factors. These are:

- the decrees of the Intergalactic Council
- the decisions made by Archangel Purlimiek and Lady Gaia about our natural world
- ancient and recent karma held within the land
- human emotions and mastery of the elements

When enough humans master their emotions and connect with the elemental spirits of the elements, we will be able to greatly influence our natural world for the highest good.

The Element of Air

All birds except ostriches, kiwis and others who cannot fly have mastered aspects of the element air. Eagles and albatrosses are examples of birds who have fully mastered this element, and they constantly demonstrate this to us. They show us that a master is able to rise into rarefied energies, see all things from a higher perspective and, most important of all, float easily on the currents of life. This is a message to all humans as well as other birds and animals.

To master air you must be able to rise beyond the collective belief in gravity. In the early part of the Golden Era of Atlantis, as already mentioned, the only way to access the Temple of Poseidon was to levitate or fly, and the High Priests and Priestesses were able to do this.

There are creatures who are here to teach us about collective beliefs. Spiders incarnated from a universe without gravity to reveal to us that mental powers can trump our collective beliefs. They build their webs in defiance of gravity by holding their vision of the finished article.

The key to mastering the air element is to connect with the unicorns, who are the beings in charge of air. They work with the elemental master Dom, who can sometimes be seen in the clouds. He has never incarnated and is ethereal. Nevertheless he commands the air elementals, who are the fairies and sylphs, and if we are open to him he can teach us about the movement and power of air.

A very simple exercise to practise is this. When you are out in nature, tune into the sylphs. If it is a still, quiet day, respectfully ask them to create a stir to move the leaves. If it is a blustery day, ask them to be calm and still for a moment. Notice how you can work with them to affect the movement of the air.

As more evolving humans take on the cloak of ascended mastery and stand in their peaceful power and equilibrium, we will be able to work with the unicorns and the elemental master Dom to blow away clouds or even calm hurricanes.

The Element of Water

Water carries the energy of love throughout the universes and this can be seen in some of the creatures who live in it.

Dolphins, who have mastered the element of water, exhibit pure joy and bliss as they enjoy the oceans of the world. They have fun and at the same time spread the love and wisdom of Atlantis to all who share the seas with them. In addition they serve by purifying the waters with their sonics, which brings angel energy into the waters.

Other fifth-dimensional water creatures are turtles, rays, whales and sharks. These all protect the angel dolphins, those who carry the wisdom of Atlantis in their energy fields. In their different ways, they have all mastered the element of water and are able to carry out their soul missions and take the knowledge and wisdom they have gained on Earth back to their star, planet or galaxy of origin.

- Dolphins originate from Lakumay, the ascended aspect of Sirius. Their soul mission is to spread the knowledge and wisdom of the great civilization of Golden Atlantis into the waters of the world, as water will hold the energetic memory imprint and pass it to us when we are ready.
- Whales originate from an asteroid in the 10th-dimensional universe of Shekinah. Their mission is to spread huge amounts of high-frequency light containing knowledge, wisdom and happiness that are currently beyond our comprehension. Again, the water will hold the energetic memory imprint.
- Turtles, originating from Jumbay, the ascended aspect of Jupiter, bring the true fifth-dimensional understanding of cosmic abundance consciousness into the world so that the waters can spread it.
- Sharks, originating from Nigellay, the higher aspect of Mars, patrol the oceans. They are the spiritual warriors who bring discipline and order to the creatures of the seas.

- In addition, huge rays from the Pleiades are individualized and fifth-dimensional. They pour heart healing into the waters.

The creatures who inhabit the coral reefs are all fifth-dimensional and they bring energy and light from Hollow Earth into the waters. These highly evolved creatures have all mastered different aspects of water and can therefore serve it with their own particular gifts. We can learn by identifying with them. If you 'swim like a fish', you are already beginning to master water. If you float on the surface, you are allowing and trusting this element to support you.

You can start your journey to mastery of water by blessing it. Every time you do so, it brings the energy of the water up to the fifth dimension and affects every creature who will subsequently shower in it, swim in it or drink it!

It helps if you identify with Master Poseidon, who is in charge of water, and his elemental master, Neptune.

The Element of Fire

Archangel Gabriel is in charge of the fire element, while his elemental master, Thor, commands the fire elementals, the salamanders.

Those who have walked on hot coals or practised fire-eating have overcome their emotions about fire, but they must be able to control this element with their thoughts in order to fully master it.

In order to practise mastery of fire, light a fire or a candle and connect with the salamanders. Then calm it right down or make it blaze with the power of your thoughts.

When you stay relaxed and commanding, you can put out house or forest fires. You can even harness the light of fire and help to spread the warmth and cheer of its flames.

The Element of Earth

Despite the fact that we walk on earth and are in constant contact with it, few humans have mastered it. However, worms, who are fourth-dimensional insects, are able to thrive within the earth! They serve by bringing the element of air into the soil.

Some brave souls have survived initiations where they have been buried alive in earthquakes or during ceremonies. They have mastered aspects of the element of earth.

Lady Gaia herself is in charge of the element of earth, and the elemental Master Taia oversees the earth elementals, the gnomes and goblins, and those who are partly earth, like the imps and pixies.

Visualization for Enjoying the Elements

1. Prepare a space where you can be relaxed and undisturbed. Light a candle if you can.
2. Sit quietly and breathe comfortably with the intention of connecting with the elements.
3. Focus upon your activated Earth Star.
4. Ask Archangel Michael to place his deep blue cloak of protection around you.

Enjoying Air

5. Imagine yourself standing on a hilltop looking out over vast spectacular views.
6. You are watching a golden eagle rising and floating effortlessly on currents of air.
7. He turns and glides towards you, inviting you to ride on his back.

8. You find yourself lying on the back of the eagle with your arms outstretched as he takes you on a journey to experience the joy, peace and exhilaration of mastering this element. Take as long as you need.
9. The eagle brings you back and you thank him.

Enjoying Water

10. Imagine yourself on a glorious white sandy beach lined with palm trees.
11. A turtle emerges from the water and walks up to you, inviting you to ride on his back.
12. He takes you into the ocean. Together you glide with the currents and surf the waves.
13. On a colourful coral reef with bright fish darting round you, you meet the other masters of water – the dolphins, sharks, rays and whales. Take your time to enjoy this experience, knowing their wisdom is touching you.
14. The turtle brings you back to the shore and you thank him.

Working with Fire

15. Imagine yourself watching a forest fire. You can feel the heat, smell the smoke and see the flickering, hot, orange flames.
16. The elemental master Thor approaches you and places his protection round you. He takes you into the flames, where you meet the fire elementals, the salamanders, who have got out of control.
17. Thor returns you to the edge of the forest where you stand calmly as a master.
18. You send out a mental blanket of calm that soothes the salamanders. They become quiet and still. The fire goes out.
19. Thank Thor and know that you have experienced mastery of fire.

Working with Earth

20. You are sitting with a huge earth dragon in the countryside.
21. The earth dragon invites you to sit on his back and accompany him along the ley lines.

22. Together you plunge deep into the earth, into a system of brightly lit underground tunnels.
23. You travel up and down, passing a portal of light. Bless it.
24. You reach a place where the tunnel has collapsed because the ley line is broken.
25. As a master of earth, you project a powerful frequency of love through the earth ahead of you.
26. You watch the ley line repair itself. Your loving mastery has prevented an earthquake or landslip on the surface of the planet.
27. The earth dragon returns you to the surface, where you relax, watching the birds, the dolphins, a bonfire and a worm moving the soil.

Facets of Enlightenment

CHAPTER 42

The Lilac Fire of Source

A new layer of the Violet Flame has been released for us – a lilac layer. Lilac is made up of violet mixed with pure white and a little of the pink of pure love. This is a flame of freedom.

The wondrous Archangel Gabriel is in charge of the element of fire, with its ability to transmute, purify, cleanse, inspire and warm. White Fire is Source light stepped down through Archangel Gabriel and his twin flame, Hope, at a ninth-dimensional frequency. This is a masculine energy. Violet Fire is the cosmic violet of Archangel Zadkiel and his twin flame, Lady Amethyst. This is a feminine light. They merge into lilac, which is a divine feminine light that gently cleanses and transmutes as it soaks softly into our energy fields. It washes out impurities with compassion yet firmness, always leaving hope and anticipation of something better.

Lilac Fire is a perfectly balanced ninth-dimensional tool for mastery and ascension. It is the highest and finest manifestation of the Violet Flame that humanity has been offered so far.

The Cosmic Diamond Violet Flame is also ninth-dimensional at its highest resonance. This is a predominantly masculine tool, for the diamond actively cuts away the old.

Archangel Gabriel's etheric retreat is above Mount Shasta, California (along with that of St Germain). Archangel Hope's is above Malaysia. Archangels Zadkiel and Amethyst share their retreat, which is above Cuba. You can connect with the Lilac Fire of Source at a central point in the triangle above these three places. When you do this, the glorious 12th-dimensional Seraphim who surround the Godhead will project their chant of manifestation into it. This adds huge potential and power to the flame, enhancing and solidifying your thoughts.

You can also invoke Lilac Fire and it will cascade into your energy fields from the ninth-dimensional realms.

You can only embody the full effect of the Lilac Fire of Source once you have expanded into higher enlightenment and illumination. Because of its power to dissolve the old and reveal purity, it can take this planet and all humanity through the process of enlightenment, mastery and ascension. St Germain, who used to be the master of the Seventh Ray of Transmutation, embodied the Violet Flame. You can embody the Lilac Fire of Source as soon as you are ready, and this decree will help to prepare you.

Decree for the Lilac Fire of Source

'I AM the Lilac Fire of Source,

I AM the Flame of Love,

I AM the Wings of Freedom,

I AM the Song of Joy,

I AM the Heart of the New Golden Age.

I AM READY. BATHE ME IN YOUR LIGHT.'

Say this three times a day and feel your light, anchoring, magnifying and expanding.

This is a very powerful decree that works under grace. Therefore you do not need permission to use it. It has the huge advantage of purifying everything it touches, then bringing it into perfect balance and harmony and filling it with love.

Mass Lilac Fire of Source Dispensations

When a number of people send this mighty energy out, it forms a vast ball of cosmic intent, which is held by the Intergalactic Council and dispensed as needed. You may call on it, for example, when an entire country has been at war or experienced internal conflict.

Every single time you think about or send this energy, it is activated and used for the highest good by the spiritual hierarchy.

Dragons and Angels

There are beautiful elemental dragons who carry the frequency of the Lilac Fire of Source. They have been waiting in Hollow Earth for it to be revealed once more and are now returning to the surface of the planet to work again with humanity. They are helping to speed the movement to the fifth-dimensional paradigm by breathing the Lilac Fire into corporations, governments, large organizations and other structures, so they can start to embrace the ethical way of living that will predominate in the new Golden Age.

As heart centres world-wide are now starting to open, the Lilac Fire dragons are also helping to transmute the energies that have been washed out. They are accelerating the process by working deeply but gently within the heart chakras of those who are ready. They then open up the space so that the new ascension energies can anchor in the hearts of humanity.

They are also waiting for us to direct them. Then they can act to clear, transmute and purify the planet and the people. At last our progress can accelerate.

Working with thousands of angels, Archangels Zadkiel and Amethyst are also co-operating on a planetary level to provide massive downloads of the Violet Flame. They work in harmony with pulses from the Great Central Sun that are designed to raise the vibration of Earth's energy very rapidly. Their task is to create a purified template into which this new higher light can move. They become very active for seven days leading up to solar events such as eclipses and coronal mass ejections, and their assistance since the Cosmic Moment has been invaluable.

Archangel Zadkiel's angels also assist many aspirants with their current lesson plan and show them light and grace to help them learn, absorb and move forwards.

They are now preparing to help the second wave of lightworkers, who have recently awoken and who will be needing guidance, cleansing and clarity for the next phase of their mission. Many of these souls have chosen to awaken during the second ascension wave. Nevertheless, in a very short space of time, they have to make big leaps in spiritual progress. Archangels Zadkiel and Amethyst are ready with the Violet Flame and the Lilac Fire of Source to ease their pathway.

Visualization to Utilize and Embody the Lilac Fire of Source

1. Prepare during the day for deep meditation. Eat lightly and ensure that you are attuned to a higher vibration by thinking about spiritual matters.
2. Set your sacred space and light a candle.
3. Invoke Archangels Zadkiel and Amethyst and the Lilac Fire of Source.
4. See the energies of the Violet Flame pouring down towards you.
5. Then, from the heights of the ninth dimension, see the pink ray of pure love leaving the Cosmic Heart portal.
6. Watch the two energies dancing and merging together above you to form a beautiful sparkling violet-pink.
7. As this light swirls above your Stellar Gateway, see vibrant high-frequency dragons and angels forming. They dance with the flow of the flames.
8. Now call this energy down into your body and fields. Allow it to integrate at the deepest cellular level, dissolving any density or issues you may have.
9. Feel it spreading through every facet of your being, lighting you up with the magic of grace, purity and love.
10. Breathe this energy out so that it starts to illuminate everyone and everything around you. See the bright violet-pink light transmuting all that is not love and replacing it with a much higher vibration.
11. Ask the dragons and the angels of the Lilac Fire to go to places that are in need of assistance.
12. Visualize armies of these beautiful beings flooding the planet with alchemizing light that allows higher possibilities to emerge.
13. Ask to embody and anchor this ascension energy permanently within your fields.
14. Thank Archangels Zadkiel and Amethyst, the dragons and the angels.
15. Return to where you are sitting and radiate the Lilac Fire to everyone in your life.

CHAPTER 43
Twin Reflections for Ascension

Twin Flames

Your twin flame is the other half of your soul and may be anywhere in the universes. These two parts are a perfect match, and if they meet, they create a non-growth relationship, because they are fully contained with each other. Because Earth is a mystery school in which to learn, souls do not generally choose relationships that do not offer growth.

There is another reason why twin flames rarely meet. During their soul journeys each flame accumulates different experiences, which causes them to resonate at different octaves. But their mutual vibration must be pitch-perfect to draw them together.

At the end of Lemuria, when the etheric beings asked Source to be allowed to experience physical bodies, each soul was allowed to connect with their twin for a brief period. One would incarnate to experience the physical world while the other would hold the light and guide from the etheric world. In some cases they then changed roles. As time passed, it was no longer considered to be the best use of the twin's energy to act as a guide, so they mutually agreed to explore different aspects of the universes.

As already mentioned, Diana's twin flame is Kumeka, who is her main spirit guide. He has never incarnated, but has remained in spirit. In this lifetime he did not find her light until she was in her thirties and they did not connect until it was time for her mission to start. Even from spirit he is a hard taskmaster, especially as he has no concept of the challenges of inhabiting a physical body!

Those who are waiting to meet their twin flame in order to ascend may have been distracted by illusion. Diana knew someone who was born on the same day as her twin flame. They met on their 16th birthday and realized they had perfectly interlocking birth charts. But they were so wrapped up in each other that they could not grow. He died when they were in their thirties because neither of them was able to expand. He then guided her from spirit so that she could at last be free to experience and expand during her physical lifetime.

Soul Mates

A soul mate is someone who emits some of the same frequencies as you do. This means you may meet several in your lifetime. Because you are resonating with some of their vibrations, you are often immediately attracted to them. They all offer lessons they have agreed to teach, and you may be drawn together for that reason. These relationships can often be very interesting but also challenging, because the lessons that need addressing are immediately brought to the surface for resolution.

Sometimes two or more soul mates may arrive in your life at the same time, offering unique challenges and opportunities for growth and love!

Because soul mates from previous incarnations are currently returning to complete any karmic residue, when these issues have been successfully navigated, the relationship can offer perfect mutual support and provide each person with the complete freedom to move forwards on their spiritual pathway.

It is very important to understand that the ascension process currently being experienced is an individual one. It is entirely down to you as the master to be fully responsible for all facets of your pathway. It is time to release the illusion that you are incomplete. One of the biggest steps to mastery is to actualize your wholeness and embrace your individual master self.

A moment of true enlightenment is when you realize the above and take full responsibility for every aspect of your journey. As mentioned earlier, the higher forces have been preparing souls to face this lesson by withdrawing their abundance of assistance. They are standing back and allowing us to flex our powers of creation and mastery. This can be disconcerting for those of us who have consciously or unconsciously relied on their guidance. It is an especially big learning opportunity for those who are sensitives, as they have often been particularly attuned to their guidance. However, the purpose of our angels and guides in withdrawing from us is to give us the opportunity to develop and use our own innate power. We must all learn to take our own decisions and create our own future.

On the ascension path, our light shines when we develop qualities such as love, compassion, understanding, patience, warmth and loyalty, and bring honour, leadership, strength and unity into all our relationships.

Visualization for Higher Relationships

1. Prepare a space where you can be relaxed and undisturbed. Light a candle if you can.
2. Sit quietly and breathe comfortably with the intention of raising the light of your sacral chakra to draw in high-frequency relationships.
3. Focus upon your activated Earth Star.
4. Ask Archangel Michael to place his deep blue cloak of protection around you.
5. Call in the pure white light of Archangel Gabriel to purify and clear your sacral chakra. Relax while he does this work.
6. Ask him to place within your sacral a shining diamond of purity. Then see the light expanding and filling your sacral with soft diamond pink.
7. Visualize a relationship based on pure love and trust. This may be a current friendship, relationship or partnership or one you wish to attract.
8. See this soft pink diamond energy expanding from your sacral and touching the sacral of the other person.
9. Picture their sacral light up with the same vibration of true love.
10. Set your intention now to manifest this in your current life and start drawing it to you.
11. Ask Archangel Gabriel to overlight this for the highest good of both of you.

CHAPTER 44

Mastery of the Law of One

A master takes full responsibility for everything and everyone in their life. They know that we draw every circumstance and person towards us.

If you have challenging people in your life, you have either attracted them or chosen them as part of a pre-life contract. You may be learning from them or you may be illuminating them with your higher understanding and love. As an enlightened master, you see into their souls and treat them with equanimity and without judgement. (That is the ideal. Even ascended masters have a little ego!)

It is the same with situations. You draw every experience to your energy fields, however unlikely this seems. Again, this is usually to learn, so it is your responsibility to look within to discern how you could have attracted whatever is showing up in your life. Remember, you may have chosen to undergo this experience in order to help others.

This understanding is hugely liberating, for if you can create a situation, you can send out energy to change it or replace it with something more satisfactory.

An enlightened master asks:

- 'How did I attract this person or situation?'
- 'What can I change within myself to transform my outer world?'
- 'Why is that person behaving like that towards me?'
- 'What can I see in their heart and soul that makes them act like that?'
- 'How can I treat them so that they feel safe with me and I light up their master self?'
- 'How best can I serve others?'

As your chakras expand and become fifth-dimensional, people treat you differently and you will notice this. Furthermore, you automatically light up their heart and other fifth-dimensional chakras so that they move onto their ascension path.

One of the tasks of an enlightened master is to demonstrate fifth-dimensional living by example. While you are in a physical body, can you maintain the higher master qualities of equilibrium, non-judgement, total truth, joy, faith, kindness, confidence and an enlightened perspective while facing life's challenges? You are asked to hold the intention to act like a master.

It is at such moments that it is helpful to call on the great Illumined Ones mentioned in this book. You can ask them to overlight you and charge up the qualities you need that are already encoded within you. This is a practical as well as inspiring way to help yourself.

Remember that as you develop these qualities of grace and integrate them into your energy fields, you will automatically offer the same service to others. You may help hundreds or thousands of souls without even being aware of it.

As we move towards the new Golden Age of Aquarius, we will once more embrace the Law of One on Earth. Everyone who lives by this spiritual law is automatically a master.

The Law of One has seven facets that enable us to live in harmony with ourselves, each other and All That Is:

1. Grace pours from the heart of Source. It dissolves all lower vibrations. The energy of grace instantly forgives and forgets, thus replacing the old with pure light. It sets us free and we can offer it to others.

2. Intention is energy that is focused on a situation to bring about the highest outcome. Because it encapsulates heart energy, it is incredibly powerful.

3. Manifestation is the ability to use the power of our thoughts to alchemize matter from light. When this is activated for the highest good of all, it is a great service.

4. Karma is a way of taking responsibility for every thought, word or action, for it all returns to us in the mirror of life.

5. Responsibility is the mark of a master who knows they are accountable for everything that happens in their life.

6. Unconditional love is an enlightened form of acceptance of all beings without judgement.

7. The Law of One is the knowing that you are within me and I am within you. This applies to all creatures. We cannot harm any sentient being, for we harm ourselves. All are part of Source and one another.

The Law of One is the template for fifth-dimensional living. When it was established during the Golden Era of Atlantis, everyone lived together in harmony and true happiness.

The blood Moon of 28 September 2015 allowed the energies to rise so sharply that instant karma returned to Earth for everyone. The spiritual hierarchy intends to use this to wake up the souls of Earth who are still asleep. As a result of this, and the rapid rise in frequency on Earth, the Intergalactic Council has decreed that the Law of Grace will also be applied to allow humanity to ascend more gently than many lightworkers anticipated.

All the souls who lived in Atlantis will remember how to live by the Law of One, as it is the unified key to a life of unity, love and bliss. Souls who are incarnating as golden children already have the ability to embrace the higher universal laws. They are arriving on Earth now to lead the way as teachers. Since the Cosmic Moment of 2012, these young Illumined Ones have had the opportunity to discard their Veil of Maya as they are born. Many of them have done so. They remember who they are.

Life here will change very rapidly over the next five to 10 years in preparation for the new Golden Age starting in 2032. The souls who are awake are leading the movement towards ascension and they are dedicated visionaries determined to bring in the new paradigm quickly.

The application of the Law of One to all on Earth is starting to bring about a beautiful change to our planet as the pupils of Earth become masters instead.

Decree to Live by the Law of One

1. 1. Prepare a sacred space where you will be undisturbed. You can choose to be outside if you wish.
2. Face the East and state aloud to the universe:

   'I, [name], walking master of light, now decree in the name of Source to live my life by the Law of One.

   I choose to walk in the beauty of grace. I choose to make intentions for the highest good of all around me. I choose to manifest all I need as I live a life of mastery. I choose to bless my life with loving karma. I choose to take responsibility for myself and my beautiful planet. I choose to love myself and others unconditionally. With these laws, I now embrace my highest enlightenment!'

3. Repeat the decree three times with power and intention.
4. Finish by stating once:

   'As within, so without. As above, so below.'

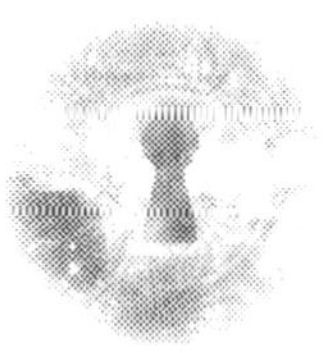

CONCLUSION

The Glorious Golden Future as an Enlightened Master

The spiritual hierarchy constantly tells us to visualize the glorious future so that we can create it. So here is a vision of our glorious golden future as enlightened masters:

- In the new Golden Age, the businesses that will thrive will be those that co-operate for the highest good and serve humanity, animals or nature.
- We will enjoy creative, satisfying work.
- We will treat children and animals as beautiful souls in our care.
- We will respect and honour nature and the waters.
- We will treat our physical bodies with care.
- When money ceases to have relevance, soul satisfaction will be the driving force behind all that we do.
- We will communicate with elementals, angels, dragons, unicorns and the masters who have preceded us.
- We will only speak words of kindness and love.

- We will give thanks for all we receive.

Walk tall as an enlightened master and influence your world to become a golden one.

ABOUT THE AUTHORS

Author photo: Wayne Lawes

Diana Cooper received an angel visitation during a time of personal crisis. She is now well known for her work with angels, Orbs, Atlantis, unicorns, ascension and the transition to the new Golden Age. Through her guides and angels she enables people to access their spiritual gifts and psychic potential, and also connects them to their own angels, guides, Masters and unicorns.

Diana is the founder of The Diana Cooper Foundation, a not-for-profit organization that offers certificated spiritual teaching courses throughout the world. She is also the bestselling author of 27 books, which have been published in 27 languages.

Tim Whild is an ascension and Lightbody expert, who has been working closely with the evolvement of Earth for most of his life.

Tim was a High Priest in the eras of Atlantis and Ancient Egypt, and is using his collective memories to bring through the spiritual gifts and information stored in those times. His current work with ancient Atlantean technologies is already helping those on a spiritual path around the world. Tim runs workshops and Skype sessions, and writes a regular blog for his co-author, Diana Cooper. This is his second book to be published in the field of esoterica.

www.dianacooper.com
www.timwhild.com

HAY HOUSE

Look within

Join the conversation about latest products, events, exclusive offers and more.

 Hay House UK

 @HayHouseUK

 @hayhouseuk

healyourlife.com

We'd love to hear from you!

Printed in the United States
by Baker & Taylor Publisher Services